BETWEE
WARS
1919–1939

The cartoonists' vision

ROY DOUGLAS

Routledge
Taylor & Francis Group

LONDON AND NEW YORK

First published 1992 by Routledge
2 Park Square, Milton Park,
Abingdon, Oxon, OX14 4RN

Simultaneously published in the USA and Canada
by Routledge
a division of Routledge, Taylor & Francis Group

711 Third Avenue, New York, NY 10017

Routledge is an imprint of the Taylor & Francis Group, an informa business

Transferred to Digital Printing 2006

First issued in paperback 2013

© 1992 Roy Douglas

Typeset in Linotron Sabon 10/12pt
by Intype, London

British Library Cataloguing in Publication Data
Douglas Roy
Between the wars 1919–1939: the cartoonists' vision.
1. Cartoons, history
I. Title
741.5

Library of Congress Cataloging in Publication Data
Douglas Roy.
Between the wars, 1919–1939: the cartoonists' vision/Roy
Douglas.
1.   p.   cm.
World politics — 1919–1932 — Caricatures and cartoons. 2. World
politics—1933–1945—Caricatures and cartoons. 3. Statesmen—
Caricatures and cartoons. 4. Wit and humor, Pictorial. I. Title.
D727.D683   1991
940.5′1′0207—dc20   91–13984

ISBN 978-0-415-04497-4 (hbk)
ISBN 978-0-415-86757-3 (pbk)

BETWEEN THE WARS
1919–1939

Contents

Acknowledgements

The author wishes to express his grateful thanks to people who have assisted materially in the work. His wife, Jean, checked the manuscript and provided many helpful suggestions, particularly for cutting out verbiage and clearing up obscurity. Professor Bertram Pockney and Mr John Taylor of Surrey University checked through the author's translations from Russian and German respectively, and provided a number of interesting sidelights which have found their way into the book. Mr David Mills was similarly helpful with the French and Italian.

The author also wishes to express his gratitude to the following: The British Library for permission to reproduce material from the Newspaper Library; the *Chicago Tribune* for permission to reproduce copyright material ('The New Menace', Cary Orr, 14 November 1918, 'While Others Talk', Cary Orr, 19 October 1924, 'Those Disquieting Sounds', Cary Orr, 29 October 1929, 'An Untrustworthy Machine', Cary Orr, 22 October 1929, 'Lessons of History', Cary Orr, 4 September 1939, 'Some Day the Worm will Turn', J. McCutcheon, 19 July 1936 – copyrighted 1918, 1924, 1929, 1939, 1936 Chicago Tribune Company); Express Newspapers plc for permission to use material from the *Daily Express*; News Group Newspapers Ltd. for permission to reproduce copyright material from the *Daily Herald*; Solo Syndication & Literary Agency Ltd. for permission to use material from the *Daily Mail*; Solo Syndication & Literary Agency Ltd. and the *Evening Standard* for permission to use material from the *Evening Standard*; the *Los Angeles Times* for permission to reproduce copyright material; the *Morning Star* for permission to reproduce copyright material; News Group Newspapers Ltd. for permission to use material from the *News of the World*; the *New York Times* and the estate of Edwin Marcus for permission to reproduce copyright material, reprinted courtesy of the Marcus family; *Punch* for copyright material reproduced by permission; the *San Francisco Chronicle* for permission to reproduce copyright material.

The author and publisher have made every effort to obtain permission to reproduce copyright material throughout this book. If any proper acknowledgement has not been made, or permission not received, we would invite any copyright holders to inform us of this oversight.

All of these cartoons have been reproduced from contemporary newspapers. The quality of the print was often poor. The author apologizes to the reader for these imperfections.

Introduction

When the First World War ended with the Armistice of 11 November 1918, the joy was almost universal. People on the Allied side had long spoken of the conflict as the 'war to end war'. Many people even in the ex-enemy countries seem to have felt considerable relief, and to have entertained high expectations that a settlement would be made in a spirit of cooperation.

It is true that there was still a great deal of fighting in the revolutionary and national wars which were deciding the fate of the former Russian Empire, and that some people hoped – or feared – that the ideas of 'Bolshevism' would spread to other countries, and overthrow existing political systems in a maelstrom of civil war. Few people, however, can have anticipated in November 1918 that the international conflict which had been raging for four years would be resumed well within the lifetime of those who participated in the carnage.

Within a short time of the Armistice, the Allied victory seemed complete. The German Emperor had fled into exile. His ministers were utterly discredited, and had been replaced by other people with very different political ideas. The defeated enemy was disarmed, shorn of territory, and required to pay large 'reparations' to the victors. The old 'Central Powers' were surrounded by countries which either had fought on the Allied side, or were new 'client states' of the victors, dependent for their very existence on Allied benevolence. All of those countries had, to all appearances, every interest in maintaining the status quo. The French army and the British navy were the strongest forces in the world.

Ten years on, at what we now know to be the approximate half-way line between the two World Wars, the position seemed even more secure. True, there had been relatively minor wars in the interval; but the new international organization for peace, the League of Nations, had played a substantial part in resolving those wars, and had won considerable prestige thereby. The United States and the Soviet Union both held back from joining the League; but those two countries were not then hostile 'superpowers' but nations far too preoccupied with their own internal business to interfere with anybody else for a very long time to come. In the 1920s, there had been international conferences which seemed to settle affairs in the Pacific area and in western and central Europe so closely that no country could disturb the peace without calling everybody else down against it. Plans were on foot for a World Disarmament Conference which every significant nation on earth proposed to attend.

How was it that this apparently secure pattern broke down, and within a further eleven years the world had embarked on a new war which was to claim five times as many lives as its predecessor? The task of studying how it all happened has been attempted many times. Unfortunately, many of the accounts have been designed rather to teach political lessons than to study how people came to act as they did. The present book is primarily concerned to examine how matters looked to the people living through them, and its vehicle is the cartoon.

Cartoons are useful for several reasons. Many of them are still funny if we understand their context, and others are still profoundly poignant. They tell us a great deal about the ideas which the cartoonists, and the people who gave space to the cartoons, were seeking to put over. In some cases, they also tell us what the governments of the countries in which they appeared were anxious for people to believe. No cartoonist or newspaper editor working in Hitler's Germany, or in Stalin's Soviet Union, would have dared to express a point of view which differed from that of the country's political leaders. In other places, there was far more freedom. In the democratic countries, and for a long time even in Mussolini's Italy, cartoons were constantly produced which were highly embarrassing to the government of the day.

A cartoon also tells us a great deal about the assumptions and ideas of the people to whom they were addressed. In no country, not even in a totalitarian country, can a cartoonist expect to make much mileage out of a cartoon which will be perceived by its readers as foolish or wicked. Thus it is possible through the vehicle of the cartoon to capture the spirit of its readers, at the particular moment in which it was drawn, with considerable accuracy.

That spirit often changed within a short time, and the cartoons tell us that it was changing. German cartoons about France change within a few years from representing 'Marianne' as a militarist armed to the teeth to representing her as the foolish dupe of the infernal machinations of the Soviet Union. During roughly the same period, the international perceptions of other countries, such as Britain, Italy and the Soviet Union, also undergo significant changes which are mirrored in cartoons.

As the 1930s advanced, the pace of events, and also the pace of changing perceptions, accelerated rapidly. In at least one cartoon here illustrated, the whole point was lost in the few days between when it was drawn and when it appeared in print; so that what was designed as a comforting assurance of national preparedness and phlegmatic resistance to panic looked like a very sick joke when the magazine reached the hands of its readers.

It is important to understand the attitudes which people in different countries were taking to events, and also the reason behind those attitudes. How was it, for example, that Hitler was followed not only by psychopaths (which is easy enough to understand!) but by decent Germans? What sort of arguments weighed with them, and eventually disposed great numbers of them to die in the Nazi cause? What did the Czechoslovak crisis of September 1938 look like to people in various countries who were living through it, or viewing it in the immediate aftermath? How was it that people whose ideas had had a strong tinge of pacifism were brought to favour policies which they must have known in their hearts were likely to lead to war? The contemporary cartoon tells us much about such matters.

The author, who teaches undergraduates, is conscious of the difficulty of explaining the world of half or three-quarters of a century ago to people living in a radically different environment. In some ways the surfeit of books and television programmes about the inter-war and wartime periods makes the task more difficult and not less so; for all too often the complex issues are presented in a simplistic manner, as a sort of developing Manichaean struggle between the forces of good and the forces of evil. Yes, there certainly were forces of pure evil at work; and it is difficult to see either the Nazi concentration camp guard, or the paranoid Stalin instigating his massacres, in any other light. Yet there were also great numbers of people in all lands whose feelings and attitudes were not wildly different from our own, whom we must try to understand, if we are to make any sense of the history of the period in which they lived. The cartoon will help us.

1

They make a wilderness . . . 1918–20

The First World War had been an utterly new kind of experience for the great majority of people whom it affected. The scale of human suffering bore no comparison with any conflict fought within living memory, save only the American Civil War of the 1860s. No less remarkable was the degree to which not only combatants, but civilians, national economies and – above all – human minds were influenced by the events. For four years the war was the centre of attention in most European countries, and eventually it became the centre of attention for countries outside the confines of Europe, notably the United States and Japan.

To many people, war was at first a thrilling, challenging experience. Pictures survive which show great crowds, mainly of young men, gathered in the principal cities of Europe to cheer their own countries' entry into the war. Recruiting offices were besieged by eager volunteers. Even amid the worst horrors of the real war which followed, deep and lasting friendships were forged. Old men who fought still often recall their experiences with a measure of sentimental nostalgia.

At the beginning, the principal belligerents on one side – generally known as the Allies – were Britain, France, Belgium, Russia and Japan. Italy joined the Allies in 1915. In 1917, Russia withdrew from the war, in circumstances to which we shall need constantly to allude; but in the same year the United States joined in on the Allied side. The other side, commonly called the Central Powers, was made up of Germany, Austro-Hungary, Turkey and Bulgaria.

Europeans and Americans were assailed by propaganda through all available media of expression. Patriotic propaganda, designed to encourage support for the various national war efforts, was countered by appeals directed by the other side towards potentially disaffected ethnic minorities. The British tried to stir up Arabs against the Turks, the Germans tried to stir up Irish against the British, the Austrians tried to stir up Poles against the Russians, the French tried to stir up Czechs against the Austrians, and so on.

There were people in all countries who, starting from very disparate ideological standpoints, regarded the war as an evil thing which should be stopped at the earliest possible moment; people who considered the restoration of peace to be more important than victory for one side. Some

1

of those people saw war as inconsistent with the Christian faith; others, of all religions and of none, refused to accept the dreadful moral burden of wilfully encompassing human death and mutilation.

There were political objectors to the war. Many Socialists had long contended that international war was fratricide among the working class; that workers, if they fought anybody, should fight the 'class enemy' at home, not members of their own class who happened to live in different countries. Many Liberals perceived that all war was likely to involve the loss of hard-won liberties, and a long check for reforms which they sought to achieve. Many Conservatives saw that war would destroy the stable and ordered relationships which they considered indispensable for human well-being.

In the United Kingdom, where the pressures were a good deal less severe than in most continental countries, there were various signs of opposition to war. Two members of the Liberal Cabinet and a junior minister resigned when Britain entered the conflict. Other prominent Liberals, and a number of parliamentary backbenchers, later began to work for peace negotiations. One leading Conservative did the same, and wrecked his career in consequence. The sessional Chairman of the Labour Party in 1914 was an opponent of the war; but he and those colleagues who agreed with him were thrust aside by other members of their party. The introduction of conscription presented many difficulties, and arrangements had to be made to permit Quakers and others who opposed the war on moral grounds to register as Conscientious Objectors. It was never politically possible to extend conscription to Ireland.

When people do particularly nasty things to each other, they usually devise highly idealistic explanations of what they are doing. Ordinary people, as well as official propagandists, had to persuade themselves that the destruction and suffering was all worth while. In Allied countries, politicians began to speak of the 'war to end war'. All the hatred and slaughter and suffering and destruction was presented as a kind of catharsis, essential for creation of the peaceful world which would assuredly follow. At the same time social injustices would be rectified; those heroes of the war who survived would receive from a grateful nation the treatment which their sacrifice demanded. We do not need to castigate the men who offered such promises, or deride them as hypocrites; in most cases, they had probably convinced themselves of the truth of what they were saying. The human power of self-delusion is almost unbounded.

The most dramatic political changes of the wartime period occurred in Russia. For the first two years of war, the Russian Empire ranked along with Britain and France as one of the principal Allied Powers. In March 1917, the Tsar was forced to abdicate, and a republic was proclaimed. The 'Provisional Government' of the Republic sought to continue the war, and many people in Britain and France viewed the change of administration with relief.

2

In the event, the new government of Russia brought no military benefit to the Allies; and in November the second phase of the revolution occurred, with a *coup d'état* by the Bolsheviks against the Provisional Government. It will be necessary to revert later to the story of that revolution, and its world-wide implications; suffice, for the moment, to say that the Bolsheviks were pledged to take Russia out of the war. In March 1918, the Treaty of Brest-Litovsk was concluded between the Bolsheviks and the Central Powers. It resulted in great tracts of the former Russian Empire passing into the hands of Germany and Austro-Hungary.

By this time, the United States had entered the war on the Allied side. In January 1918, President Wilson set out his celebrated 'Fourteen Points' which, he judged, should govern the peace settlement. In so far as those points were specific they were moderate indeed, and they were shot through with a strong idealism, very much the President's own. Yet Wilson spoke only for himself. He had no authority to speak even for the American Congress, still less for the other Allies.

In the first part of 1918, the cards seemed stacked in favour of victory for the Central Powers, provided only that they could finish the war before the almost limitless reserves of American manpower were fielded. After their triumph in the east, a serious effort was made to win a similar victory in the west. The German 'spring offensive' of 1918 was held by the Allies; but it was touch-and-go. This was followed by a long period of hiatus; but then, in the autumn, the Central Powers collapsed quite suddenly. First Bulgaria and then Turkey sought and obtained armistices from the Allies. Late in October, the Austro-Hungarian Empire began to fall to pieces, and on 3 November it concluded an armistice – while the process of internal disruption continued. A few days later the German Emperor decided that the war was lost, and fled. On 11 November the German armistice was signed.

When wars of the past had come to an end, the belligerents sought to make peace as quickly as possible, in order that everyone could regulate his life under the new state of affairs. That arrangement had usually worked, because the spokesmen of victors and vanquished alike were small minorities, and there was no real 'public opinion' which could hold them to account.

The same course was followed again. The Paris Peace Conference opened on 18 January 1919, less than ten weeks after the fighting ended. All the public pressures were still for revenge. The draft treaty of peace with Germany was presented on 7 May, and signed at Versailles on 28 June. The treaty with Austria was signed at Saint-Germain in September, the Treaty of Neuilly with Bulgaria in November. The treaties with Hungary and Turkey took rather longer, but both of these were concluded in 1920.

What principles governed the peace treaties? The map of Europe was to be redrawn. The new territorial definitions were based on several different ideas which commended themselves to the victorious Allies. Nationalism prescribed the establishment of states each roughly corresponding with a single nationality or a small group of closely related nationalities. Economics prescribed that the new states should each contain a range of different resources and means of production. Strategy prescribed that they should be limited by geographical features which were difficult to cross. A sense of history prescribed that they should correspond with units which had existed in the past. Overriding all of these considerations was the rule 'woe to the vanquished', which required that the defeated enemy should in no circumstances stand in a better position than he had been in before the war. Unfortunately these various ideas were frequently in conflict, and almost any frontier which could be justified on one principle could be condemned on another.

The territorial settlement was to some extent predetermined by promises which had been made during the war, and by the more or less openly declared interests of the victorious Powers. France bitterly resented the amputation of Alsace and Lorraine which had followed the Franco-Prussian war of 1870–1, and successfully demanded restitution. Belgium enforced an ethnic claim to a much smaller slice of German territory. The German coal-producing area of the Saar, contiguous with France, was separated from Germany for fifteen years, at the end of which time a plebiscite would be held to decide its eventual fate. The Rhineland – the part of Germany lying between the Rhine and the French frontier, along with a few bridgeheads to the east – was set under protracted Allied occupation.

President Wilson's 'Fourteen Points' had included the promise of an independent Poland with access to the sea. This seemed reasonable enough, for Poland had been partitioned between Russia, Prussia and Austria in the late eighteenth century, and the Poles were plainly anxious to see their country restored. Access to the sea was imperative; but where could that access be granted? In a large part of eastern Germany there was a mixed population, German and Polish. Eventually the so-called 'Polish Corridor' was created, coming to the sea at Gdynia. Gdynia, however, could not handle all of Poland's overseas trade, and so the ethnically German town of Danzig (now Gdansk) was cut off from Germany and established as a 'Free City', controlled by the League of Nations but linked economically to Poland. Thus Germany was split into two parts, separated by the Corridor and Danzig. The smaller part, centring on Königsberg (now Kaliningrad), became known as East Prussia. Memel (now Klaipèda) was also cut from Germany as a 'Free City', but it was soon incorporated in Lithuania.

Other parts of Germany – the northern part of Schleswig and part of Silesia – were eventually cut off, in response to the will of their inhabitants. Before the war Germany had had a number of colonies. These had probably been of little value to Germany, and they had certainly been administered with much brutality. All were given as 'Mandates' to various Allied countries.

If Germany sustained serious territorial losses, not all of which were justified on ethnic grounds, Austro-Hungary fared much worse. Three new sovereign countries emerged from the wreck: Austria, Hungary and Czechoslovakia, while large territories passed to Italy, to Poland, to Romania and to the new country Yugoslavia. The Ottoman Empire managed little better. The Arab lands of the Levant became either independent or else 'Mandates' of Britain and France, while much of European Turkey passed to Greece.

Financial reparations were demanded of the defeated enemy. In Britain, not the most revengeful of the victors, a substantial overall majority of the House of Commons joined in telegraphing Prime Minister Lloyd George in April 1919, to deplore 'reports . . . that the British delegates, instead of formulating the complete financial claims of the Empire, are merely considering what amount can be extracted from the enemy'. In the end, the Allies' attempt to extract reparations was to prove a most dubious benefit to the Allies even in the short run, while it would prove a major irritant to international relations, and a substantial encouragement for the later rise of Hitler.

Germany was to be disarmed. Conscription would be abolished, the army reduced to 100,000 men, and the air force relinquished. The German navy would be drastically reduced, and the submarine force lost entirely.

President Wilson's 'Fourteen Points' had included a proposal to establish an international organization to secure peace in the future. Here was the germ of the idea of a 'League of Nations'. The principle was generally accepted by the Allies – but not by the United States itself. Wilson encountered increasing difficulties with his own country, and by the time peacemaking was complete the United States had opted out of the idea of the League, and had practically repudiated all responsibility for enforcing the peace settlement. America withdrew into truculent isolation from the affairs of Europe, but continued to demand settlement of the enormous 'war debts' incurred by her erstwhile Allies.

Many people in the defeated countries were disposed to believe that they had not really been defeated at all, but had been cheated by an offer of terms when victory lay within their grasp: terms which were dishonoured by sharp practice of the Allies.

That view was later argued with much savagery and exaggeration by the Nazis, but it was not without a small grain of substance. Wilson's 'Fourteen Points' were the most authoritative statement of Allied war aims available at the time of the Armistice, even though – as we have seen – they did not formally commit the government of any country. The peace which eventually emerged was a good deal less generous than the 'Fourteen Points'.

The Allies were in serious dispute with each other even before peace was signed, and they soon fell into still more savage quarrels. By the immediate aftermath of the peace treaties, the European Allies were united by little more than a common apprehension of German recovery, a common resentment against the American demand for payment of war debts, and common fear of the political implications of Russian Bolshevism. Even these bonds of union rapidly began to disintegrate. The new countries thrown up by the war and its aftermath learnt very quickly the vices of older countries, such as military aggression and economic nationalism. The Americans soon decided that they had been brought unnecessarily into war by European machinations, while the Europeans were currently attempting to renege on their duty to pay for the indispensable help they had received from the United States.

Thus did the victory of 1918 turn to dust and ashes. There was still hope that peace might be preserved so long as memories of the sufferings and privations remained vivid. Perhaps, when those memories at last faded, sheer habit would take over, and people would accept the new arrangements simply because they were familiar.

Cartoon 1.1 Der Grosse Baal. *Simplicissimus*, Munich, 2 July 1918

„Herr, dürfen wir nicht Frieden schließen?" — „Erst zahlen!"

A few months before this German cartoon was drawn, Russia had been forced to make the humiliating Peace of Brest–Litovsk with Germany and Austro-Hungary. This great victory of the Central Powers had been followed by the military 'spring offensive' in the west. When the cartoon appeared, at the beginning of July 1918, Germany was known to be preparing another great offensive. Even at this late date, many Germans still entertained hopes not merely of averting defeat, but of securing a clear victory over the Allies.

The cartoon comments on the relationship between the Allies. President Wilson of the United States, 'the great Baal', is being worshipped as a god by Marianne (France), and by King George V of Britain. They implore him to allow them to seek peace. Wilson replies, 'First pay!' The implication is that the European Allies would gladly make peace with the Central Powers, but were being kept in the war against their will by the financial power of the United States.

There is no reason for thinking that the governments of Britain and France were at that moment anxious for 'peace at any price', as the cartoon suggests. They had contrived, though with considerable difficulty, to hold the German offensive which had been launched earlier in the year. On the other hand there can be little doubt that they would have looked at matters very differently if the United States had not entered the war on their side a year or so earlier. Nor was there doubt that America's economic power was massive, and that the European Allies were already deeply indebted to her.

It is rather striking that the British representative chosen for the cartoon was not a leading politician or soldier but the King. The King's role in British affairs was by this time largely ceremonial; but many Germans, who were familiar with monarchs exercising real power, probably did not appreciate that fact, and credited him with a great deal more power than he actually possessed.

These two cartoons appeared in the spring of 1919, while the Paris Peace Conference was in session, but before the Treaty of Versailles had been signed with Germany. They illustrate popular attitudes in Britain and France at the time.

The expression 'Der Tag' was well known in Britain. It was widely believed that German officers before 1914 used to toast 'The Day' when their country would embark on a victorious war against Britain.

In this cartoon, 'Der Tag' takes on a very different significance. Allied statesmen are gleefully administering unpalatable peace terms to a reluctant type-cast jackbooted German. The 'Big Four' Allied leaders shown are (from left to right): Prime Minister David Lloyd George of Britain, Prime Minister Vittorio Emmanuele Orlando of Italy, Prime Minister Georges Clemenceau of France, and President Woodrow Wilson of the United States. The German is firmly grasped in a hand whose fingers bear the names of the five principal Allies. The Allies are administering the 'pill' with visible delight. They no doubt hope that it will produce better German behaviour in future, but they also seem to be taking considerable pleasure in Germany's immediate discomfiture.

The label on the box – ' "Big Four Pills" – worth millions a box' – alludes to a very famous advertisement of the period, in which a certain brand of pills was described as 'worth a guinea a box'. This testimony derived, allegedly, from a lady who was impressed with the efficacy of the pills. A guinea (£1.05) was in those days a very considerable sum of money.

The French cartoon, 'Easter 1919', shows Clemenceau offering an

Cartoon 1.2 Der Tag! *Daily Express*, London, 7 May 1919

DER TAG!

Cartoon 1.3 Pâques 1919. *Le Canard Enchaîné*, Paris, 23 April 1919

PAQUES 1919

– J'en veux pas, de ton œuf. Y a rien d'dans!

Easter egg to Marianne, who contemptuously refuses it – 'There's nothing in it!' Perhaps Marianne was disappointed that the peace settlement had not yet been concluded; more probably, she was disappointed that the terms which seemed likely to emerge from the Conference were not more beneficial to herself.

Cartoon 1.4 The reckoning. *Punch*, London, 23 April 1919

THE RECKONING.

GERMAN: 'MONSTROUS, I CALL IT. WHY, IT'S FULLY A QUARTER OF WHAT *WE* WOULD HAVE MADE *THEM* PAY, IF *WE'*D WON.'

Two profoundly different views of the question of 'reparations'. Under the Treaty of Versailles (28 June 1919), Germany was required to pay reparations to the Allies for the damage she was held to have done to them during the war. The sum was not fixed by the Treaty, but the principles on which it was to be assessed were laid down. As with other elements of the Treaty, the essentials of the Versailles provisions were known and discussed long before the Treaty was signed.

The British cartoon, 'The reckoning', is from *Punch* – a journal which, while satirical, was addressed to an educated, and presumably 'responsible', readership. It is a savage comment on German protests at the reparations terms which were being discussed.

Cartoon 1.5 Trost. *Simplicissimus*, Munich, 24 June 1919

Cartoon 1.5, 'Consolation', is an equally bitter reply. The German mother assures her starving child that 'when we have paid 100,000,000,000 [marks], then I shall be able to give you something to eat'.

Both cartoons are, no doubt, exaggerations, although there was real hunger in Germany in the immediate aftermath of the war. The British cartoon implies that Germany was getting off lightly, and protesting unreasonably; while the German cartoon is indicative of the resentment felt over the matter. It is not difficult to see in both cartoons, and in the two preceding ones as well, something of the feelings which prevailed around the time of the peace settlement, and were to bedevil international relations in the years which followed.

Cartoon 1.6 In troubled waters. *John Bull*, London, 3 May 1919

IN TROUBLED WATERS.

Orlando leaving the Ark.

The preceding four cartoons comment on ill-feeling between the ex-Allies on one side and the defeated enemy on the other. These two cartoons emphasize ill-feeling between the ex-Allies themselves, and show that Germany was by no means the only country to feel deeply aggrieved. Both cartoons concern the question of Fiume (now Rijeka). The problem must be understood in its context.

Italy entered the war on the Allied side in 1915 as the result of a secret treaty (the so-called Pact of London) and in pursuit of what was unashamedly called 'sacro egoismo'. She expected to gain a large part of the Austro-Hungarian Empire, some (the South Tyrol) adjacent to modern Austria, and other parts (Venezia Giulia) at the head of the Adriatic and along part of its eastern seaboard. Among the anticipated territorial gains was the town of Fiume, whose own population was largely Italian, but whose hinterland was Slav.

France, who wished to strengthen the new country which was being formed out of Serbia, Montenegro and the South Slav parts of Austro-Hungary, preferred that Fiume should pass to that country – which is now known as Yugoslavia. The United States, of course, was not at war

Cartoon 1.7 Fiume. *Simplicissimus*, Munich, 29 July 1919

Fiume
oder Die lateinischen Schwestern   (Zeichnung von O. Gulbransson)

In Erbschaftsangelegenheiten soll es bisweilen unter den nächsten Anverwandten zu kleinen Meinungsverschiedenheiten kommen.

at the time of the Pact of London, and President Wilson refused to be bound by its terms. The French view seemed to be prevailing, and in April 1919 the Italian delegates left the Peace Conference in high dudgeon. The British cartoon shows Wilson, captain of the 'Peace Ark', trying to induce Orlando to return, instead of trusting himself to the obviously unseaworthy vessel, 'Fiume Claim'. 'Will ye no come back again?' is the refrain of a well-known Scottish song, alluding to 'Bonnie Prince Charlie'.

The German cartoon, 'Fiume, or the Latin sisters', shows Italy and France fighting furiously over the Fiume question. The caption is to the effect that a small difference of opinion has arisen about a matter of inheritance.

A kind of compromise later emerged, but there was further serious trouble over Fiume a year or two later.

The explanation of this cartoon provided by the *New York Tribune* brings out the sense of alienation which Japan was also feeling at the time of the Peace Conference.

Japan, who had long been closely associated with Britain, entered the war on the Allied side in August 1914, and was represented at the Peace Conference. The cartoonist's point may perhaps be related more directly to Japanese internal politics than to international affairs, but the picture brings out a feeling among Japanese who, like the Italians, considered that their country was not being accorded the importance it deserved by the major peacemakers.

Both countries were thus in an ambivalent position after the peace settlement. They had made substantial territorial gains at the expense of the Central Powers, and were naturally anxious that those countries should not become able to challenge those acquisitions; yet they also felt considerable grievance against the major Allies.

Cartoon 1.8 Japan, suppliant or defiant? *New York Tribune,*
12 June 1919

JAPAN, SUPPLIANT OR DEFIANT?

This cartoon from the Tokio "Jiji" protests against Japan's position at
the peace conference. The caption reads: "It's there, the empty seat. Why
doesn't he take it?" This comment is added: "We have heard of five great
powers of the world, and we are to be treated above the average. There is
something strange in our delegate, who assumes the position of a petitioner
begging to be treated as an equal."

Cartoon 1.9 Their turn next. *Daily Express*, London,
10 May 1919

THEIR TURN NEXT.

The fate of the other Central Powers attracted a good deal less attention in Britain, France and the United States than did the fate of Germany. In this British cartoon, however, the artist reminds them that they, too, could expect little mercy from the Allies.

The notice on the wall of the waiting room by the surgery of the Allied dentists says that gas will not be used: in other words, that no anaesthetic will be provided. At that time, nitrous oxide gas was the commonest dental anaesthetic.

As Germany emerges from treatment, the Allied dentist shouts that the patient should 'call again in 15 days'. Draft peace terms had just been presented to German plenipotentiaries, and they were given a fortnight to consider the matter – a period which was later extended.

The other 'patients' were all due to suffer heavily for their defeat. The Austro-Hungarian Empire had already broken to pieces. The treaty with Austria was signed in 1919, the treaty with Hungary in the following year. By those treaties Czechoslovakia became an independent state, while large areas of former Austro-Hungarian territory passed to Poland, Romania, Yugoslavia and Italy. Turkey lost all of the Arab lands which had belonged to the Ottoman Empire, including Syria, the Lebanon, Palestine, Arabia and Mesopotamia (Iraq). These places came under varying degrees of French or British control. Much of the area which Turkey still retained in Europe was handed to Greece. Bulgaria lost some territory to Yugoslavia. All of the ex-enemy countries were largely disarmed.

16

Cartoon 1.10 Peace and future cannon fodder. *Daily Herald,* London, 17 May 1919

PEACE AND FUTURE CANNON FODDER

The Tiger: "Curious! I seem to hear a child weeping!"

This cartoon, surely one of the most prescient ever drawn, appeared in the Labour *Daily Herald* in May 1919. Allied peace terms had been presented to the German delegates, but had not yet been accepted, when it appeared.

The 'Big Four' emerge from the Peace Conference, headed by Georges Clemenceau of France who acquired the nickname 'the Tiger', which is used in the caption, because of the skill with which he demolished a number of French governments. The delegates are (from left to right): Lloyd George, Orlando, Clemenceau and Wilson.

Clemenceau says to the others, 'Curious! I seem to hear a child weeping!' Behind a pillar is the weeping child, over whose head are the words '1940 class' – that is, the class of people who would be of military age in 1940.

Orlando had ceased to be Prime Minister of Italy by the time the Treaty of Versailles was signed, but was still Prime Minister when this cartoon appeared. He looks a good deal younger here than he does in Cartoons 1.2 and 1.6. Perhaps the cartoonist based his drawing on an old picture.

Cartoon 1.11 Handle with carelessness. *New York Tribune,*
20 June 1919

Handle With Carelessness

(Copyright, 1919, New York Tribune Inc.)

At the American congressional elections of November 1918, just a few days before the Armistice, President Wilson's Democratic Party lost control of the Senate. Relations between President and the Republican Senate deteriorated, and it is probably fair to say that the fault did not lie exclusively on either side. The dispute was very important for all countries, as the international commitments in which the President was hoping to involve the United States required approval of Senate.

This cartoon was drawn in June 1919, and is sympathetic with the President rather than his critics. Senators opposed to Wilson are treating a range of international problems in an irresponsible manner, kicking or throwing the President's proposals down the steps from the Capitol building in Washington – while an apprehensive Uncle Sam hides behind a tree. In the rear, the formidable Republican Senator, Henry Cabot Lodge, prepares to jettison the League Covenant – that is, the instrument designed to impose international obligations under rules of the League of Nations.

Cartoon 1.12 The gap in the bridge. *Punch*, London, 10 December 1919

THE GAP IN THE BRIDGE.

British reactions to the American Senate's decision to repudiate the League of Nations idea were varied. Both of these cartoons come from British weekly periodicals which were non-party, but would probably be called 'right-wing' in their tendency; but the messages they impart are very different.

Punch, which was sympathetic with the League of Nations idea, observed with regret 'the gap in the bridge' which Wilson had designed. Uncle Sam rests indolently on the keystone which must be set in place in

Cartoon 1.13 Jilted! *John Bull*, London, 29 November 1919

order to make the whole structure functional. The cartoon seems to imply, however, that the omission may later be repaired.

John Bull sympathizes strongly with the American decision to keep out of the League of Nations, and approves of Uncle Sam's decision to jilt the new international organization, which is drawn as an ugly and unpleasant-looking harridan. The artist probably hoped that the American action would frustrate the whole venture, and enable Britain also to escape from obligations to the League.

Cartoon 1.14 Hail and farewell. *Punch*, London, 20 April 1921

HAIL AND FAREWELL.

THE LEAGUE OF NATIONS (*making her first use of the long-distance telephone to America*). 'IS THAT MY FRIEND MR. WILSON SPEAKING?'

PRESIDENT HARDING. 'NO – QUITE THE REVERSE. RING OFF!'

[President HARDING's first message to Congress comprised a repudiation of the League of Nations.]

In the autumn of 1919, President Wilson's health failed; but the gravity of his condition was not generally realized, and he remained in office. The combination of an ailing President and a hostile Senate boded ill for any kind of consistent American foreign policy, but supporters of the League continued to hope that the next batch of elections, which were due in November 1920, would produce a strong President and a sympathetic Congress, both supporting the League of Nations idea and full-scale American participation in world affairs.

These hopes were dashed. The 1920 elections gave the Republicans control of both Houses, and the Presidency as well. The new President, Warren Harding, was deeply opposed to the idea of America joining the League of Nations. As soon as Harding settled in office, the new policy became clear. It is sometimes said that the United States withdrew into isolation. That is not true. America had far too many international interests to do that, whatever she might have wished; but she strenuously resisted all pressures to take on military commitments.

This *Punch* cartoon notes these developments with regret. The technological improvements with which the political events are linked are significant; but it will be observed that the telephones look very primitive, and that transatlantic conversations were still seen as very much a novelty.

Since the Second World War, critics of United States foreign policy have usually complained that American governments have intervened too much in the affairs of other countries. During the inter-war period, the usual criticism was exactly the reverse.

2

Revolution, 1917–21

When Tsar Nicholas II was deposed in March 1917, and a 'Provisional government' set up, Russia was in a ferment of ideas. A number of the political groups – notably the Bolsheviks, the Mensheviks and the Social Revolutionaries – would be called 'socialists'. Most of those people were disposed to support the Provisional government, at least for the time being. Had not Karl Marx argued that socialism would arise from the contradictions inherent in advanced capitalist societies? Most of Russia had not yet reached the capitalist stage of development, and so the correct course for Marxists to adopt was to cooperate with the 'bourgeois' or capitalist parties.

In the following month, the German government took the fateful step of enabling the Bolshevik leader Vladimir Ilyich Ulyanov, commonly known as Lenin, to travel through their country from his Swiss exile to Russia. The German motive was clear enough. The Provisional Government was continuing to prosecute the war on the Allied side. Lenin, it was hoped, would pull Russia out of war, whereupon the Germans would be free to deal with the western Allies.

Lenin soon overcame the scruples of his fellow-Bolsheviks about the duty of Marxists to cooperate with the 'bourgeois' parties. Russia herself was perhaps not ripe for socialist revolution; but a revolution in Russia could provide the spark which would start the conflagration of world revolution in countries like Germany, or Britain, or France, which were ripe.

The next stage, then, was to overthrow the Provisional Government. This was achieved by the so-called 'October Revolution'* in Petrograd (St Petersburg, for a long time known as Leningrad) when the Bolsheviks took control. After some initial difficulty, the Bolsheviks concluded with Germany and Austro-Hungary the Treaty of Brest-Litovsk in March 1918, and Russia withdrew from the war. Large parts of the Russian Empire were occupied by the Central Powers, while others became, in name at least, independent.

Conditions in the former Russian Empire were chaotic for years. Revolutionary and counter-revolutionary armies were organized, while many

---

* October by the old Russian calendar; November by the calendars of other countries

places on the fringe of the Empire sought to establish themselves as independent states. For years it was impossible for anybody to foretell with confidence which states were likely to emerge, what their geographical limits would be, and what political complexions they were likely to adopt.

While the First World War was in progress, the belligerent countries on both sides probably cared little about such matters. Their overriding concern was whether Russia would participate in the war or not. The Germans, as we have seen, were quite willing to encourage Lenin, whatever his long-term designs for their own country might be, because they had good reason for thinking that he would try to withdraw Russia from the war. The Allies, on the other hand, were anxious to bring down the Bolsheviks – not primarily because of any ideas the Bolsheviks might have about the internal organization of Russia or other countries, but because the Bolsheviks wanted to make peace with the Central Powers. Allied troops were therefore landed in Russia in order to help defeat the Bolsheviks, and the 'wars of intervention' began.

When the First World War came to an end, there was an immediate revolutionary surge in the defeated countries. Their governments were discredited by defeat, and their peoples were suffering great privations occasioned by the war. At that moment, however, the various revolutionary movements appear to have had little central direction or coordination with each other.

In Germany, the so-called 'Weimar Republic' was set up, within which the Social Democrats became, and long remained, the largest single political party. In one part of Germany, the erstwhile kingdom of Bavaria, a serious attempt was made to establish what would today be called a more 'left-wing' socialist state. A more formidable and general movement of extreme socialist complexion, the 'Spartacists', seemed at one moment to threaten the structure of the new German republic, but they too were beaten down – partly by the force of their enemies but also, one might say, because their ideas had not struck deep roots in German society. In Hungary an attempt was made to establish a revolutionary republic under Bela Kun. But 'red terror' was succeeded by 'white terror', and in the end Admiral Nicholas Horthy took charge, with the title of Regent – though for whom was far from clear. Horthy was to remain in office until 1944.

Meanwhile the complex struggle within the former Russian Empire continued – stirred up to a considerable degree by forces of the former Allies, who played a substantial part (though probably not a vital part) in supporting some of the national and counter-revolutionary forces which were in operation. Nowhere was the struggle more intense than in Poland.

At the end of the war, Poles were determined to re-establish their country, which had been partitioned by Prussia, Austria and Russia together in the late eighteenth century. The almost simultaneous collapse of the three great empires gave them the opportunity of achieving this, and they were much encouraged by the thirteenth of President Wilson's 'Fourteen Points', the establishment of a Polish state with access to the sea, which has already been noted. The Poles faced immense difficulties. In the first place, their country had been under different kinds of alien rule for more than a century. In the second place, there was great doubt among Poles, as among other people, as to what the geographical limits of Poland ought to be. If we define a Pole as somebody who spoke Polish as his main language and thought of himself as a Pole, then there was an undeniably Polish area centring on Warsaw; but in all directions from this nucleus there were large numbers of 'ethnic Poles' living alongside people who thought of themselves as something else – Germans, Czechs, Ukrainians, Byelorussians, Russians, Jews or Lithuanians. An appeal to the historic frontiers of Poland was of little more use than an appeal to ethnology, for historic Poland had varied enormously in its geographic area. At its extreme limit it had covered not only Poland in the narrow sense, but also most of the modern Ukraine, Byelorussia and Lithuania.

In the west, as we have seen, the 'Polish Corridor' was carved out of Germany, to give the country access to the sea. Many Germans were included, against their will, in Poland; but, conversely, many Poles remained, against their will, in Germany. In the east, the problems were even more severe. The Allied Supreme Council soon defined a line westwards of which the Poles should certainly be authorized to organize their state; but there was no implication that the Poles should not include places further east as well.

War soon broke out between the Poles and the Bolshevik 'Red Army'. First the Poles swept eastwards, and at one stage occupied Kiev – where, incidentally, there was a substantial Polish community. Then the Red Army swung back. The British Foreign Secretary, Lord Curzon, proposed that the Allied Supreme Council Line should be the line of cease-fire. Thenceforth, the line was known as the Curzon Line, and acquired great importance many years later. For the time being, however, the cease-fire suggestion was ineffectual, for both sides rejected it. The Russians advanced to the vicinity of Warsaw, where in August 1920 they were held and repulsed by the Poles. The Battle of Warsaw is still regarded by some people as one of the great 'decisive battles of history'. Early in the following year, peace was made between Russians and Poles, following roughly the line of the Second Partition of Poland in 1793. Under this arrangement, Poland extended well east of the Curzon Line, but stopped far short of the limits of historic Poland.

Poland was not the only state to be carved from the western margins of the Russian Empire during the period of the revolutionary wars. Finland and the three Baltic States – Estonia, Latvia and Lithuania – became independent. Romania secured Bessarabia. Other parts of former Russia – the Ukraine, the Transcaucasian states and the Far Eastern Republic –

remained independent for a little while; but all were incorporated during the 1920s in what became known as the Soviet Union.

Allied troops were gradually withdrawn; but the idea of 'world revolution' which had lain at the centre of the Bolshevik insurrection in 1917 did not quickly disappear. In 1920, the 'Communist International' was set up, with headquarters in Moscow, and Communist Parties were speedily organized in other countries. These parties, in theory at least, were revolutionary, and they certainly followed extremely closely the political lead of the Soviet Union. In some countries, Communist Parties were made illegal. In France and Germany, they secured large support from members of the old Socialist Parties, and a long, bitter struggle developed between the two movements. In other places, like Britain and the United States, Communist Parties never made substantial headway, although from time to time they exerted influence over people in other parties.

Thus, throughout the inter-war period, events were to a large extent overshadowed by memories of the revolutionary period around the end of the First World War. A great many people believed that the idea of world revolution was only quiescent, and had been in no sense abandoned by the leaders of the Soviet Union. Others felt great bitterness towards the 'counter-revolutionaries' who had sought to destroy, and had succeeded in containing, the revolutionary ideas which flourished at the end of the war. Each side could point with accuracy to the many wanton atrocities committed by the other. All wars are horrible, but civil wars are usually the most horrible of all. The Bolsheviks sought to destroy not merely those individuals who acted in support of the 'counter-revolutionary' cause, but also those who belonged to social groups which were regarded as 'class enemies'. An apparatus of secret police and terrorism, far more extensive and efficient than anything which had existed in pre-revolutionary days, was soon set up.

The Soviet Union was not regarded by either its sympathizers or its opponents as an 'ordinary' state. It was widely seen either as the model which all should copy, or else as the epitome of evil and world subversion. Recollections of what had happened, or what was supposed to have happened, during the revolutionary period profoundly influenced attitudes both of governments and of ordinary citizens to world events for many years to come.

Cartoon 2.1 Sud'ba ministra inostrannykh del Tereshchenko.
Pravda, Petrograd, 13 November (31 October, old style)
1917

СУДЬБА МИНИСТРА ИНОСТРАННЫХЪ ДѢЛЪ ТЕРЕШЕНКО:

Союзные капиталисты предполагаютъ...

Россійскій пролетаріатъ располагаетъ...

This Russian cartoon appeared just a few days after the 'October Revolution' (6–7 November 1917). It comments on impending changes in Russian foreign policy. The title reads, 'The fate of Foreign Minister Tereshchenko'.

Tereshchenko, who had been Foreign Minister in the 'Provisional Government' under Kerensky, is shown as a marionette, whose strings are being pulled by French and British capitalists – but who is about to be cut down by the arm of the Russian workers. The poem underneath reads,

> The Allied capitalists propose . . .
> The Russian* proletariat disposes.

The policy of the 'Provisional Government' had been to cooperate with Britain and France in the war against Germany. The cartoonist implies that Russia had by this time become no more than a puppet of capitalists from those countries.

The Russian script used in this cartoon follows the old orthography, which was later altered to the Soviet orthography which is used today.

---

* The adjective is not the ordinary modern word for 'Russian', but means more strictly 'from the Russian empire'.

Cartoon 2.2 Delezh piroga. *Pravda*, Petrograd, 5 December (22 November, old style) 1917

Дѣлежъ пирога.

'Sharing the pie' is another comment of the Russian revolutionaries on the foreign policy of the Allies. Diplomats are carving puddings labelled 'Turkey' and 'Persia'. Highly secret negotiations had been in progress earlier in the war, involving Britain, France, Russia and, to an extent, Italy, proposing the establishment of 'spheres of influence' in substantial parts of the Middle East. These negotiations were disclosed to the world when the Bolsheviks took power.

This German cartoon, 'The English friend', comments bitterly on the British decision to stage military intervention in Russia, with the object of keeping the Russians fighting against Germany. The Russian peasant, peacefully ploughing his land, is followed by a sinister lean sower, who is casting seeds in the furrows. He resembles a common German representation of John Bull, but also has the horns and hooves commonly associated with Satan. He is not sowing grain, but harmful seeds. The legend reads, 'The Devil sows weeds in Russian soil'.

Cartoon 2.3 Der englische Freund. *Simplicissimus*, Munich,
1 October 1918

Der englische Freund

(Zeichnung von O. Gulbransson)

Der Teufel sät Unkraut in russische Erde.

Cartoon 2.4 Kurt Eisner I. *Simplicissimus*, Munich, 3 December 1918

„Mein Vorgänger Ludwig I. hat München zur schönsten Stadt Deutschlands gemacht. Ich mache es zur feeleſten!"

By the constitution of the German Empire of 1871–1918, component states retained a very large degree of autonomy. This was particularly true of the kingdom of Bavaria.

A day or two before the German Armistice, a group of socialists, headed by the journalist Kurt Eisner, took power in Bavaria, deposed the King and proclaimed a republic. Not long afterwards elections were held in which the instigators of the coup were defeated. There followed a great deal of disorder in Bavaria, in the course of which Eisner was murdered.

In this cartoon, drawn during the brief period of socialist control, Eisner is mounted on a lugubrious-looking lion, and carries a flag, which is red in the original picture. The bearers of the old Bavarian royal arms were two lions, and in the centre of the shield were lozenges resembling the pattern on the lion's flank.

Eisner has a quasi-regal title, 'Kurt Eisner I', presumably suggesting that he was making ridiculous pretensions to something like royal authority. The legend underneath reads, 'My predecessor Ludwig I made Munich the most beautiful city in Germany. I am making it the most free.'

The 'Spartacist' movement in Germany was led by a group of extreme socialists, of whom Karl Liebknecht and Rosa Luxemburg are the most famous. The Spartacists took their name from Spartacus, who led a revolt of Roman slaves in 73–71 BC, a revolt characterized by much brutality on both sides, which was eventually suppressed with extreme savagery.

The Spartacist movement flourished briefly in many parts of Germany, and closely imitated the Russian pattern, by setting up local 'soviets', or councils, composed of members of putatively revolutionary social groups. There was much fighting, in which elements who today would probably be designated 'Communists' and 'Fascists' took part on the two sides. Both Liebknecht and Luxemburg were killed – perhaps murdered – and the movement was eventually suppressed.

This cartoon, 'Spartakus', was drawn while the movement still posed a serious challenge to the authorities of the new German republic. A man, whose features resemble those of Liebknecht, is attempting to saw off the branch on which he sits, an activity with predictable results. The implication seems to be that the Spartacists are attempting to sever their own movement from the body of Germany. The wording at the bottom reads, 'We mean to show the world that the people also have the right to do stupid things.'

Many cartoonists have from time to time used the figure of somebody sitting on a branch while attempting to cut it off from the tree in order to ridicule people of whom they disapproved.

Cartoon 2.5 Spartakus. *Simplicissimus*, Munich, 17 December 1918

„Wir wollen der Welt beweisen, daß auch das Volk das Recht hat, Dummheiten zu machen."

Although Cartoons 2.6, 2.7 and 2.8 were drawn in different countries at a time when wartime hatreds were still very much alive, they make very similar points.

The American cartoon appeared only three days after the Armistice. In a 'David-and-Goliath' situation, 'Freedom' has vanquished 'Militarism' (i.e. the Allies have defeated Germany); but 'Bolshevism', with a blood-soaked dagger and a flaming torch, threatens to destroy 'Freedom' in the very moment of his victory.

'Bolshevism' is constantly shown as a terrible threat in cartoons of the period. Sometimes it is 'personalized' as Lenin; sometimes it is represented as a mad-looking revolutionary, usually with unkempt hair and beard, and often with a bomb, a dagger, a flaming torch or some other weapon of destruction.

The German cartoon asks, 'How will the *Entente* decide? For Wilson or Lenin?' Wilson is drawn as a kind of angel of peace, Lenin (not a good likeness!) as a crazed axeman-pyromaniac.

The word '*Entente*' in the German cartoon derives originally from the *Entente Cordiale* reached between Britain and France in 1904. The term passed into German, as into English. The Allies of 1914–18 were often spoken of as the '*Entente* Powers'.

The German cartoon contrasts the almost idyllic peace offered by Wilson's 'Fourteen Points', and the President's earlier call for 'a peace without victory', with the perceived alternative of Bolshevik terror and destruction. In the event, neither Wilson nor Lenin 'decided the *Entente*', for the eventual peace treaties had little in common either with Wilsonian idealism or with Bolshevism.

Cartoon 2.6 The new menace. *Chicago Tribune,*
14 November 1918

THE NEW MENACE

Cartoon 2.7 Wie wird die Entente entscheiden?
Simplicissimus, Munich, 4 February 1919

Cartoon 2.8 Prince Charming and the sleeping beauties. *Daily Express*, London, 3 April 1919

PRINCE CHARMING AND THE SLEEPING BEAUTIES.

In the British cartoon the 'Big Four' – Lloyd George, Clemenceau, Orlando and Wilson – occupy the role of the 'sleeping beauty' of the familiar fairy story, and rest peacefully in their bed. The man who is about to awaken them, however, is not the handsome and romantic 'Prince Charming', but an evil-looking figure carrying a club and a bomb and bearing the word 'Bolshevik' on his brow, who is entering at the window. His somewhat incongruous garb suggests that the cartoonist may have intended him to double for the war-god Mars, or perhaps as a barbarian invader of the Roman Empire.

Cartoon 2.9 A Russian-German alliance? *Bystander,*
London, 30 April 1919

A Russian-German Alliance ?

MEPHISTO LENIN PROPOSING TO GERMAN GRETCHEN
BY LOUIS RAEMAEKERS

This cartoon makes a point which probably underlay many political and diplomatic attitudes of the inter-war period. There are parallels with the Faust legend: Lenin, as Mephistopheles, attempts to tempt the 'German Gretchen'.

Historically, the various German states had frequently been enemies of Russia; but Russian and German governments had also at times been drawn together in common interests: against Poland in the eighteenth century, against Napoleon in the early nineteenth century, and in the *Dreikaiserbund* later in that century.

At the time when this cartoon was drawn, the political systems of the two countries were developing on very different lines, and many Germans had deep fears of 'Bolshevik' subversion in their own country. Yet the two countries undeniably had some powerful interests in common. Both were apprehensive of the claims which a renascent Poland might make against them. Both were currently on bad terms with the Allies; Germany as the defeated country on which the Allies were preparing to wreak revenge, Russia as the advocate of world revolution. The victors were from time to time conscious that, if they pushed too hard against Germany and Russia, they would be likely to drive them together into a formidable amalgam.

Cartoon 2.10 Pan Paderewski macht mobil. *Simplicissimus,*
Munich, 19 May 1920

„Überall nichts als Friedensschalmeien. Ich muß wieder starke Klänge ins europäische Konzert bringen."

The first of these cartoons is headed 'Pan Paderewski gets moving'. Paderewski, the most famous pianist of his day, briefly became Premier, and for a longer time Foreign Minister, of Poland. The word 'Pan' was not his Christian name (which was Ignacy) but a Polish word meaning, roughly, 'gentleman', 'squire' or 'lord', often used in a pejorative sense.

Paderewski, driving his grand piano like a fighter aircraft into the heavens – it has guns in front – declares that he intends to make a noise in the 'Concert of Europe' to combat the talk of peace. The term 'Concert of Europe' was commonly used in the nineteenth century to refer to the major European powers, and carried the implication that those powers

42

Cartoon 2.11 Finis Poloniae. *Simplicissimus*, Munich, 4 August 1920

Von Foch gar feurig aufgeblasen.   liegt er nun traurig auf der Nasen.

had more interests to unite them than to divide them. In this cartoon, the sense is rather that Poland proposes to play an important part in European affairs.

When the cartoon was drawn in May 1920, Poland had already acquired the 'Polish Corridor' under the Peace Treaties, to the great resentment of many Germans. She was currently engaged in fighting against the Red Army, and had occupied Kiev, although war had not yet been declared formally between the two countries. Thus Paderewski had certainly 'got moving', although the cartoon seems to imply that there was something faintly ridiculous about what his country was doing. Most students of Paderewski would probably agree that his skill as a musician far exceeded his skill as a politician.

The second cartoon, 'The end of Poland', appeared early in August, when the tables had been turned, and the Red Army was advancing towards Warsaw. In the first panel, the French Marshal Foch is inflating the figure of a bellicose-looking Pole, who fearlessly confronts the Russian bear. In the second, the bear has advanced and deflated the Pole, who 'now lies sad on the ground'.

The French government had certainly given considerable encouragement to the Poles, both in their claims against Germany and in their current fighting against Russia. They deplored the Bolshevik revolution in Russia and had no confidence in the strength of the new Soviet Russia, so they had a powerful interest in establishing a strong Poland as an eastern ally.

The cartoon implies that there was never anything of substance in Poland, whose apparent power and importance was the product of French bluff.

Despite the fear of Russian Bolshevism which *Simplicissimus* frequently showed, the cartoonist seems to be quite pleased that Poland is apparently about to be destroyed by Russia. It is interesting to speculate what would have happened to Germany if the judgement that Poland was finished had proved correct.

In the event, the Poles turned at bay, just as the Red Army had done a few months earlier, and the Battle of Warsaw in August 1920 proved to be a great Polish victory.

This *Punch* cartoon approves of the new turn of events. The Bolshevik, impressed by the unexpected display of Polish strength, accepts the need for an agreement between the two countries. There is now no question of 'bolshevizing' Poland; the only question is where the frontier between Poland and the Soviet Union should be drawn. The eventual solution was a compromise between extreme Russian and extreme Polish claims.

Cartoon 2.12 The Polish hug. *Punch*, London, 13 October 1920

THE POLISH HUG.

BOLSHEVIST. 'YOUR ATTITUDE CONVINCES ME, KAMERAD, THAT WE WERE MEANT TO BE FRIENDS.'

Cartoon 2.13 But what will people say? *Daily Mail*, London, 18 March 1921

BUT WHAT WILL PEOPLE SAY?

JOHN: " You're not going to shake hands with him, are you ? "
DAVID: " Oh ! dear no, not regularly. *Only with his left hand !* "

British attitudes to the emerging Soviet Russia were far from clear, and even within Lloyd George's Coalition Government some remarkable differences could be observed. Winston Churchill was a strong advocate of military intervention. Lloyd George, on the other hand, was quite willing to come to terms.

This cartoon appeared in the *Daily Mail* in March 1921. The *Daily Mail* was a Conservative newspaper which at one time had strongly supported Lloyd George's Coalition; but its proprietor, Lord Northcliffe, was currently on bad terms with the Prime Minister, and the newspaper was becoming increasingly critical. Lloyd George had been working towards a trade agreement with Russia, which was the subject of much public discussion.

Lenin holds in his right hand the unacceptable 'red regime' in Russia, and in the other 'tainted gold' – implying that the economic assets which had been taken over by the Soviet government did not morally belong to them. David Lloyd George shows interest in 'shaking hands' with Lenin. John Bull is shocked at the idea, but the Prime Minister cynically reassures him. Lloyd George is quite willing to take economic advantages which will give him access to the 'tainted gold', but has no intention of adopting the 'red regime' which Lenin holds in the other hand.

By the time this cartoon appeared, relations between Soviet Russia and the 'capitalist' countries were beginning very gradually to settle down. Although Russia still saw herself as the natural instigator of the impending 'world revolution' and other countries perceived the latent threat, it was becoming increasingly plain that neither side was likely to do much about it for a very long time to come. If the Bolsheviks had hoped to engineer an early 'world revolution', they had failed; but so also had the opposing countries failed to disrupt the revolutionary process in Russia. Although Russia was regarded by all governments, and probably by most ordinary people, in non-Communist countries as a 'moral enemy', increasing numbers of people on both sides saw merits in trade agreements non-aggression agreements, and other similar arrangements.

3

Mediterranean problems, 1919–23

In the early 1920s, a series of disputes affected the northern shores of the Mediterranean. Some of these disputes were resolved, though not in a manner wholly pleasing to those affected; others had repercussions which persisted long after.

The Ottoman, or Turkish, Empire had entered the war in 1914 on Germany's side. In Greece, there was a protracted dispute between the King, who favoured neutrality, and some of the leading politicians, who wished to intervene on the Allied side. In 1917, the politicians won, and Greece went to war. By the Treaty of Sevres in 1920, the Ottoman Empire not only lost its Arab lands to British and French influence, but was also required to cede to Greece nearly all that remained of 'Turkey-in-Europe', save for the city of Constantinople (Istanbul). Greece also obtained control of Smyrna (Izmir) on the Anatolian mainland for a trial period.

The dispute between Greece and Turkey had roots quite as deep as the dispute between Poland and Russia, and the two disputes had many features in common. Both had strong religious overtones: Roman Catholic versus Russian Orthodox in one case, Moslem versus Christian in the other. At one time, the area which is now called Turkey had belonged to the Greek-speaking Byzantine Empire, just as large parts of the Russian Empire had once belonged to Poland. There was no clear definition of what area should become 'Greece', any more than there existed a clear definition of 'Poland'. Greeks, like Poles, were scattered over a wide area, often living in separate communities, alongside people from other ethnic groups. In Turkey, as in Russia, defeat in war encouraged a strong revolutionary movement, headed by people who desired to establish a modern, secular state.

Neither Greeks nor Turks liked the Treaty of Sèvres. Many Greeks had not ceased to hanker after Constantinople, historic capital of the Byzantine Empire, and perhaps after other parts of Turkey which still had substantial Greek populations. The Turks resented the Greek presence in Thrace and Smyrna. Both sides prepared for war, and sporadic fighting started almost immediately the treaty was signed.

The erstwhile Allies could not ignore the Graeco-Turkish war. There were considerable differences between the British and French governments – and, indeed, within the British government itself – as to what attitude the major Allies should take in the matter. Eventually, however, a new settlement was achieved by the Treaty of Lausanne in 1923. This did not entirely favour either side, and it was followed by massive population exchanges. Great numbers of Greeks were driven from Turkey, and Turks were driven from Greece. By this time the Turkish Sultanate had been abolished, and a republic headed by Kemal Atatürk had come into existence.

In the central Mediterranean, the Fiume question was by no means solved when the town was made a 'Free City'. In 1919, it was seized by an irregular band of Italians, headed by the poet and adventurer Gabriele d'Annunzio. D'Annunzio's action, and the regime over which he presided, set important precedents for Fascism. His forces were eventually driven out by the Italian authorities in 1921, but this probably weakened the moral authority of democratic government in Italy. In 1924, an agreement was reached between Italy and Yugoslavia, under which most of the town passed to Italy.

In Italy itself, a series of unstable governments was followed by King Victor Emmanuel III's invitation to the Fascist leader Benito Mussolini to form a government, in October 1922. This was associated with the so-called 'March on Rome' of Fascist mythology.

A considerable period elapsed before the new Italian government took on the worst aspects of 'Fascism', as the word is now understood, but there were early signs of chauvinistic nationalism, exemplified by the Corfu Incident of 1923. Several Italians were murdered while attempting to determine the border between Greece and Albania. Italy retorted by bombarding and seizing the Greek island of Corfu. The island, however, was soon relinquished in response to diplomatic pressure, and agreement was reached between the two countries.

Although these various Mediterranean events had alarming aspects, they also had one important positive feature, for their eventual settlement was determined not by the relative military strength of the disputants, but by international agreements, in some of which the League of Nations played a substantial part. Faith in 'the League' as a peace-keeping organization was an important feature of international politics in the 1920s and early 1930s, and at the time there were substantial grounds for that faith.

Cartoon 3.1 The seat of war. *Daily Express*, London,
23 June 1920

THE SEAT OF WAR!

This cartoon appeared in mid-1920. Mars stirs up the growing dispute between Greece and Turkey. The 'seat of war', however, is the British taxpayer. The implication is that the two sides are only able to strike warlike attitudes towards each other because they are receiving financial assistance which ultimately derives from the British taxpayer.

About this time, an active campaign was developing in a section of the British press for 'economy', and strong pressure was being put on the government to cut down expenditure in all directions, but particularly in overseas commitments.

Cartoon 3.2 L'enfant terrible. *Punch*, London, 7 July 1920

L'ENFANT TERRIBLE.
YOUNG TURK. 'I WILL FIGHT TO THE DEATH FOR OUR NATIONAL HONOUR.'
OLD TURK. 'WELL, IF YOU MUST. BUT I WASH MY HANDS OF THE WHOLE BUSINESS – UNLESS, OF COURSE, YOU WIN.'

The term 'Young Turk' was not a new one in 1920, when this cartoon appeared. It was applied to a particular movement in Turkey, but also more widely as a general term for critics of the Sultanate, who sought both internal reforms and a policy of vigorous nationalism.

'Young Turks' objected very strongly to the Treaty of Sèvres, which had recently been signed by their country's government, which ceded nearly all the non-Turkish parts of the Ottoman Empire, and also substantial areas which could be considered ethnically Turkish.

Cartoon 3.3 Petit capricieux. *Humanité*, Paris, 24 September 1922

PETIT CAPRICIEUX   par H.-P. GASSIER

Raymond — « Et puis, non, j'veux pas qu'on joue à la guerre, moi ...voilà ! »

As the Graeco-Turkish war developed, considerable differences could be discerned between attitudes of the French and British governments. The Lloyd George Coalition (or at least its Prime Minister) was a good deal more disposed to give positive encouragement to the Greeks than were the French.

The disposition of the British to favour a 'forward' policy in Asia Minor where the French were more hesitant could be contrasted sharply with the 'forward' policy of the French towards Germany in the Ruhr, which the British were resisting, a matter which will be considered more fully in a later chapter.

In this cartoon, Lloyd George (on the left) wishes to 'play at war' in Asia Minor, while the French Premier Raymond Poincaré, the 'capricious child', who is clutching more peaceful toys, retorts petulantly, 'No, I don't want to play war with you, so there!'

Cartoon 3.4 La guerre en Asie Mineure. *Telegraaf*, Amsterdam, reprinted in L'Europe Nouvelle, Paris, 7 October 1922

LA GUERRE EN ASIE MINEURE

Le Grec: "Meurtrier!"
Le Turk: "Incendiniare!"
... cependant qu'ils sont tous deux armes pareillement ...

(Extrait du "Telegraaf")

This is a Dutch cartoon reproduced in a French periodical. The Greek addresses the Turk as 'Murderer!', the Turk retorts by calling the Greek 'Arsonist!' The cartoonist comments, 'Meanwhile they both act in a similar way.' Each carries a burning torch and a knife or sword.

This cartoon was perhaps unfair on the Greeks, whatever the rights and wrongs of the original dispute. The incident which evidently prompted it was the recent Turkish capture of Smyrna – a town which then had about a million inhabitants, half of whom were Greeks. The Turks had massacred those Greeks on whom they could lay hands, and had set the town on fire.

Cartoon 3.5 Fashisty trebuyut rospiska Ital'yanskovo parlamenta. *Pravda*, Moscow, 30 August 1922

Фашисты требуют роспуска итальянского парламента

Муссолини (вождь фашистов) "Подвиньтесь,
Ваше Величество! Я тоже умею
действовать по-королевски. "

This Russian cartoon appeared in August 1922, shortly after Mussolini had taken power in Italy and demanded the dismissal of the Italian Parliament.

Mussolini (a very bad likeness!), dressed as a brigand, pushes the King aside on his throne. He says to Victor Emmanuel, 'Move over, Your Majesty! I also can act like a king!'

Although Mussolini was still a very long way from claiming the measure of dictatorial power which he later exercised in Italy, he was already arrogating to himself a good deal more power than past Italian Prime Ministers had possessed.

Cartoon 3.6 Fascisten. *Simplicissimus*, Munich, 22 November 1922

Blaſt kräftig nur hinein — 'nein — 'nein.
Italia muß größer ſein!

This cartoon is based on the famous statue which portrays Romulus and Remus being suckled by the legendary she-wolf.

The Fascists in the cartoon, however, are not feeding from the wolf's udders, but are blowing air into them. One of them is saying to the other, 'Just blow with all your might, it is necessary that Italy should get bigger!' The implication is that they are attempting to make Italy appear more important in world affairs, not by adding anything of substantial value but by mere wind.

Cartoon 3.7 La flotte italienne bombarde l'île de Corfou. *Le Canard Enchaîné*, Paris, 5 September 1923

La flotte italienne bombarde l'île de Corfou

The Italian sailors bombarding Corfu in 1923 are mounted on gondolas and dressed as gondoliers.

The cartoon may be meant to suggest that the Italian venture was an absurd reaction to the putative insult to national honour presented by the murder of Italian representatives who had been assisting in demarcation of the Graeco-Albanian frontier.

Perhaps a deeper meaning is also intended, for the gondoliers are clearly Venetians. Corfu, and other islands along the eastern side of the Adriatic, as well as many places much further east, had once belonged to the Venetian Republic. The current Italian interest in Corfu was probably related, in part, to the idea that Italy was rightful heir to the assets of historic Venice.

Cartoon 3.8 Evropa mozhet spat' spokoyno. *Izvestiya,*
Moscow, 7 September 1923

ЕВРОПА МОЖЕТ СПАТЬ СПОКОЙНО.

After the Italian bombardment and seizure of Corfu, the Greeks appealed
to the League of Nations.

This Russian cartoon was drawn almost immediately afterwards. The
title is 'Europe may sleep calmly'. The absurd man in evening dress who
is attempting to extinguish a serious blaze with a wash-bottle of a type
used in chemistry experiments bears a flag above his hat, 'League of
Nations. Bodyguard of Europe against the danger of fire'. The implication
is plainly that the League is completely inadequate for the task confronting
it.

As it happened, the League was far from ineffective. Later in September
1923, it prevailed upon Mussolini to withdraw from Corfu, and eventually
it produced a settlement which required, among other things, that Greece

should compensate Italy for the crime which had been the cause, or pretext, of the Italian action against Corfu.

In this period, and for a good many years afterwards, the Soviet government considered the League of Nations as, at best, a useless organization – and, at worst, a device established by the 1918 victors to retain their international ascendancy.

4

Reparations, 1919–25

In the aftermath of the First World War, a mass of different, but to some extent related, problems led to profound instability in Germany.

Political parties had long existed in Germany, and before the war the Reichstag had been elected on a very wide franchise; but the Reichstag had only very limited powers, and therefore the politicians who led those parties had no experience of truly responsible office. In 1918, the traditional centres of power were deeply discredited by defeat, and the politicians suddenly found themselves vested with real power, but in circumstances in which almost anything they did was bound to come under bitter and largely irresponsible criticism. They found themselves widely blamed for defeat itself, and for almost everything which went wrong in Germany thereafter. The temptation for people who had no confidence in the new republic or its institutions to make every ounce of political capital from the situation was irresistible.

Germans, like people in other countries, had been fed with their own government's propaganda, and probably believed, on the whole, what they were required to believe. The suddenness of the German collapse after the extremely strong military position in which the country stood a very few months before the Armistice made it difficult for people to appreciate what had happened, and it was much more satisfying to believe that the country had been betrayed by internal traitors and compelled to accept a savage, shameful and vindictive *Diktat* imposed upon them by the malice and trickery of the Allies. The Nazis later exploited that mood to the limit, but the mood was there before the Nazis appeared on the scene.

The war had been very costly to Germany in every way. Enormous numbers of Germans had died or been mutilated, apparently in vain. At the end there was considerable hunger among the civilian population. In Germany, as in most European belligerent countries, there had been massive war spending, which had been partly financed by inflation and other dubious financial expedients. The temptation for any government to go on inflating thereafter in order to meet its accumulated debts was hard to resist. On top of this was the enormous, and uncertain, burden of reparations to be paid to the Allies.

The international argument over the related questions of war debts and reparations ran on for more than a decade. Broadly speaking, the other Allies all owed money to the United States, while Germany owed money in reparations to the European Allies. Britain was in a somewhat ambivalent position, as creditor to the Europeans and debtor to the Americans. There was also a difficult question affecting Russia. Before 1917, the Russians had fallen heavily in debt to the European Allies. The Bolsheviks repudiated those debts, although at one point they seemed prepared to repay some of them. The particularly vigorous anti-Bolshevism witnessed in France appears to have been based to some extent on the fact that a great many Frenchmen in quite modest circumstances had followed their own government's advice in pre-war days and invested heavily in Russia.

There was a further complication in that considerable debts existed at one time between Germany and Russia. These debts, however, were annulled by agreement at the Treaty of Rapallo in April 1922. By that date, there did not seem to be any serious danger of Russian-inspired Communism subverting the German state, at least for a long time to come. The Germans and the Russians had no serious immediate grievance against each other, while both had considerable grievances against the major Allies, and also against Poland, which had made large territorial encroachments against both of them.

The reparations story was also influenced by the vagaries of French politics. In France, political parties were not for the most part as sharply defined as in Britain and the United States, but nevertheless substantial groupings could be discerned. In the first post-war elections, in 1919, the anti-socialist *Bloc national* secured a substantial overall majority. In the following year, 1920, Clemenceau made an unsuccessful bid for presidency of the Republic, and shortly afterwards resigned as Premier. Paul Deschanel, who had defeated Clemenceau, went into a mental home a few months later, and was himself succeeded by Alexandre Millerand, original architect of the *Bloc*. Millerand at first attempted to make the presidency a real source of power, but in the end his functions became largely honorific. Thus within a short time two of the most prestigious French politicians disappeared from the central arena.

Clemenceau's immediate successor as Premier was the relatively inconspicuous Georges Leygues, but in January 1921 he was succeeded in turn by Aristide Briand, now widely regarded as one of the most impressive and also conciliatory of French inter-war politicians. Briand found himself caught between the bitterly anti-German passions of the *Bloc* and the growing disposition in Britain and the United States to favour a more moderate policy towards the former enemy. After a year in office, Briand was replaced by Raymond Poincaré.

Poincaré was seen by many of the *Bloc*'s sympathizers as a kind of 'man of destiny'. He had been President of the Republic from 1913 to 1920. An aloof and not very likeable man, but with an unusual reputation for personal integrity, Poincare was to dominate French politics from the early part of 1922 until the *Bloc*'s electoral defeat in 1924. This period witnessed the most intense dispute over the reparations question.

The most crucial event of the dispute was the occupation of the Ruhr. In November 1922, the Germans, who were in the throes of intense economic difficulties, sought a moratorium on reparations payments. In January 1923, the French and Belgians sent troops into the Ruhr, Germany's industrial heartland, ostensibly to protect a mission of engineers, but in practice to enforce reparations. To this the Germans retorted with a general strike in the Ruhr. In order to support their compatriots in this action, the German government permitted inflation, which had reached unprecedented levels even before the Ruhr crisis, to continue without limit.

French occupation of the Ruhr was to continue until 1925. Both the French and the German positions are today understandable. The Germans protested that their economy was in ruins, and steadfastly denied that their own position during the war had been morally worse than that of anybody else. In German eyes, their country was paying an unjust price for defeat, not a just price for special wickedness. The French pointed to the devastation which their country had suffered at German hands during the war, and also pointed out that they were still being required to repay war debts to the United States and Britain. Britons and Americans largely sympathized with the Germans in the current crisis, seeing the Ruhr occuaption as a simple act of international aggression. Many people in both countries began very seriously to question whether they had been right to fight on France's side during the war.

Even more baleful than the immediate crisis were its long-term implications. In Germany, anti-French anger was intense, and it was augmented by the widespread ruin fostered by inflation. Enormous numbers of people found their life-savings reduced to nothing in a short space. It was very tempting for such people to accept simplistic 'solutions'. To those 'solutions', and their frightful implications, it will be necessary constantly to return.

Cartoon 4.1 Die ausgeplünderte Germania. *Simplicissimus,* Munich, 21 April 1920

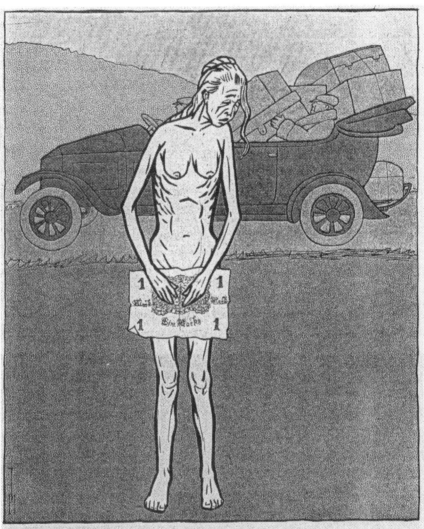

„Alles haben mir meine Söhne verschoben. Nur eine lumpige Papiermark ist mir geblieben, um meine Blöße zu bedecken."

'Plundered Germania' bemoans her fate. 'My sons have squandered everything. Only a tattered paper mark is left to hide my nakedness.' A prosperous-looking passenger speeds by, in a car laden with trunks full of reparations seized from Germany by the Allies.

The cartoonist is complaining both about reparations and about the depreciation in value of the mark. Before the war, it had been backed by gold; but wartime and post-war inflation have left merely the 'tattered paper mark'.

In the spring of 1920, a single paper mark still had some purchasing power. The time would soon come when it was, literally, not worth the paper on which it was printed.

Cartoon 4.2 'Permanent occupation'. *Daily Herald*, London, 10 March 1921

The French government soon began to complain that the reparations due from Germany were not being paid, and considered the possibility of military occupation in the industrial Ruhr to enforce payment. In this cartoon, French Premier Aristide Briand is discussing the idea with a general. He attempts to entice him with the prospect of 'another Ireland – and all our own!'

In early 1921, a large part of Ireland was in a condition of virtual civil war, as many Irish people sought independence from Britain. The struggle appeared at that moment interminable – 'permanent occupation' by the British, in fact. The cartoonist implies that French occupation of the Ruhr would produce a similar result for France.

As it happened, most of Ireland secured effective independence in the following year; but the struggle over the Ruhr continued longer, and had even more dire implications. Briand, who is here represented as something of a fire-eater, would soon look like a model of moderation.

Cartoon 4.3 The efficiency experts. *Star*, London, 3 May 1921

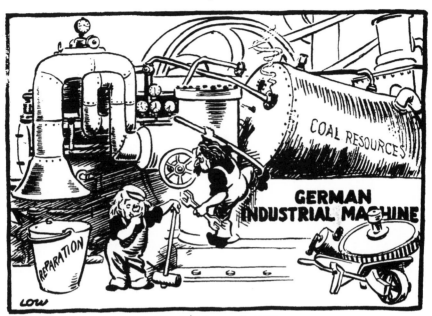

The Efficiency Experts.

" Half a minute! I wonder if removing bits of the machine really does speed up production.''

Even during the period of Briand's premiership in 1921, differences could be discerned between the approaches of British and French governments to the question of German reparations.

A number of British commentators, including the economist Maynard Keynes, had already begun to make very serious criticisms of the peace treaties, objecting to them not so much on the ground that they were hard on Germany, but that they would ultimately prove harmful to the economy of every country, victors as well as vanquished.

This cartoon does not challenge the whole idea of reparations, but it questions the way in which France was proposing to enforce those reparations. Briand is in the process of disconnecting Germany's coal resources in the Ruhr from her industrial machine. Lloyd George, the other 'efficiency expert', doubts whether this will accelerate the production of reparations.

The cartoonist David (later Sir David) Low, was highly critical of the domestic policy of Lloyd George's government during this period, but he obviously sympathizes with the Prime Minister's approach to the reparations question. The two heads of government are presented – correctly – as men who were on quite good personal terms, despite occasional disagreements on policy.

Cartoon 4.4 'Stop!' *Simplicissimus*, Munich, 26 February 1922

"Bevor du einen neuen anfängst, bezahle erst deinen alten Krieg!"

Cartoon 4.5 Antanta. *Pravda*, Moscow, 6 September 1922

Антента – entente cordiale (по-русски сердечное согласие)

Two periodicals with very different political tendencies note the rapid deterioration of France's relations with her erstwhile Allies during the period of Poincare's ministry, which commenced in January 1922.

In the *Simplicissimus* cartoon, Poincaré, in military uniform and with drawn sword, is mounted on a war-horse. He is confronted by Uncle Sam, with a long list of France's war debts, who tells him, 'Before you start another, pay for your last war!' The implication is that Poincaré's policy involves a serious risk of starting a new European war.

The *Pravda* cartoon, '*Entente*', explains to its readers the meaning of the term '*Entente Cordiale*' in Russian. Lloyd George and Poincaré are in furious battle, while the space around them is littered with memoranda, notes and questions relating to their many differences.

Lloyd George, and other British ministers who came into contact with Poincaré, were on bad personal terms with him. Anglo-French relations did not improve significantly in October 1922 when Lloyd George's Coalition Government fell, and was replaced by the Conservative administration of Bonar Law.

Cartoon 4.6 Gutenberg und die Milliardenpresse.
Simplicissimus, Munich, 15 November 1922

The problem of inflation in Germany rapidly grew worse. In the *Simplicissimus* cartoon of April 1920 (Cartoon 4.1), the 'tattered mark' still had some purchasing power, and afforded some cover for Germania's nakedness.

In this cartoon, which appeared in the same magazine in November 1922, the fifteenth century German printer Gutenberg, inventor of the movable type, stands back in horror from the printing press churning out banknotes which are then being grasped by eager hands. 'This I had not intended,' he protests.

The banknotes emerging from the printing press in the cartoon are mostly of the thousand-mark denomination. A thousand marks would have been worth about £50 before 1914 – perhaps twenty or thirty times that sum in present-day pounds. In mid-October 1922, marks were being exchanged at about 12,000 to the pound.

The German economy was in dire straits. In October 1922, the British proposed a five-year moratorium on reparations payments, which was rejected by the French.

Within a few months after the cartoon was drawn, the German press would be printing banknotes with face values in milliards – thousands of millions – of marks. At one point a postage stamp could cost up to 50 milliard marks, and people were rushing out to buy goods immediately after they received wages, because the money they held would have diminished substantially in value a few hours later.

Cartoon 4.7 Dettes de guerre. *De Amsterdammer*,
Amsterdam, copied in *L'Europe Nouvelle*, Paris,
9 December 1922

DETTES DE GUERRE

L'Allemagne supporte la France, qui supporte l'Angle-
terre, pendant que l'oncle Sam domine cet échafaudag"
branlant.

(Extrait du « De Amsterdammer.»).

The French insistence on reparations, despite the appalling plight of Germany, is not wholly attributable to greed or to 'revanchism'. The French
were under pressure to pay war debts to Britain and the United States.
Britain in turn was heavily indebted to the United States.

It is easy to understand how each creditor, conscious of pressure from
others, was unwilling to relax its claim against debtors. The Americans,
who were the general creditors, tended to argue that they had been
brought into the European war, in which their own interests were scarcely
involved, and received little gratitude from the Europeans, who now sought
to avoid obligations which they had freely incurred. The maximum ill-
feeling was generated, which made all forms of cooperation difficult, and
easily tempted all countries into economic policies of narrow nationalism.

Cartoon 4.8 The vulture. *Star*, London, 11 January 1923

THE VULTURE: "Righto, Poinc., I'll take your message, but I'll come home to roost."

A remarkably prophetic cartoon, which appeared the day after the French government had informed Germany of its intention to occupy the Ruhr.

Poincaré despatches the vulture 'Revanche' – 'Revenge' – in lieu of a pigeon to Berlin. The vulture agrees to take the French message, but promises to return to roost. That promise was amply fulfilled.

The French decision generated enormous bitterness, not only in Germany but in Allied countries. In years to come, many people in Britain and other countries who might have been expected to sympathize with France's military and diplomatic problems in face of the rising threat of Hitler's Germany recollected the Ruhr invasion, and were quite willing that the balance between France and Germany should move in favour of the latter.

71

Cartoon 4.9 L'hiver dans la Ruhr. *Le Canard Enchaîné*, Paris, 17 January 1923

L'HIVER DANS LA RUHR

Nos troupes sont fraîches et joyeuses, mais on pèle de froid ... Envoyez du charbon ...

The German government embarked on a policy of non-cooperation with the invaders. The Ruhr coal-owners were forbidden to supply coal to the French and Belgians.

'Winter in the Ruhr' is a French satirical comment. A French officer writes home that his troops are in good heart, but freezing. He asks for coal. The irony is that the Ruhr was one of the principal coal-producing areas of Europe.

German coal-owners supported their government's action. About a week after this cartoon appeared, six of them were tried by court-martial for disobeying orders of the occupying authorities, and received only fines. The German mark began to collapse catastrophically, as the authorities financed striking Ruhr workers through further inflation.

Cartoon 4.10 Fair play gegen Deutschland. *Simplicissimus*, Munich, 30 April 1923

Ist das englisch?

The German, helpless and tied to a tree, is being kicked by a negro wearing boxer-shorts carrying the French insignia. He complains to a sympathetic-looking John Bull, 'Is that English?'

As we have seen, the French invasion of the Ruhr was widely deplored in Britain, where people were disposed to think that Germany had already suffered enough, and any further punishment would be counter-productive.

The fact that the man assaulting the German is a negro and not (as one might expect) a white Frenchman is significant. At that date, most Europeans knew very little about negroes from personal experience, but had been encouraged to regard them as inferior to white people. Thus the negro in the cartoon has a half-simian appearance. A number of coloured troops from the French African colonies were included among the forces occupying the Ruhr. This was seen at the time not so much as an assertion that France took an enlightened attitude to racial equality, but rather as a studied insult to the Germans.

There was a disposition on the part of the French authorities to use coloured troops for duties which were certain to be particularly resented by the Germans. Thus, not long before this cartoon appeared, more than a hundred railwaymen's families were turned out of their houses on to the streets by French colonial troops. The cartoonist may well have had that incident particularly in mind.

Cartoon 4.11 Notre ami héréditaire. *Le Canard Enchaîné,* Paris, 22 August 1923

'Our hereditary friend' is a French comment on the decline of good feeling between British and French people in the period 1914–23. The word 'hereditary' seems to be sarcastic.

In 1914, the British 'Tommy', who has come to fight alongside the French against Germany, is greeted enthusiastically by the French population. In 1923, the Englishman travelling in France is ostracized by the French people because of the deep quarrel over the Ruhr.

Perhaps the cartoonist is trying to remind his French readers that France had had good reason to be grateful to Britain in the past, and that current French policy in the Ruhr, which ignored British as well as German susceptibilities, was neither grateful nor wise.

Cartoon 4.12 Poincaré et l'Allemagne. *L'Action Française*, Paris, 7 November 1923

POINCARÉ ET L'ALLEMAGNE

Les Boches de Paris. — Ces discours, quelle scie !

The French occupation of the Ruhr had considerable repercussions for French politics. This cartoon is from a very 'right-wing' and pro-Poincaré periodical. Poincaré's political opponents are represented as 'les Bosches de Paris' – i.e. the Paris Germans – and a message of affection for 'Germania' has been carved into the trunk. The figures in the tree include Louis Malvy (top, centre), Joseph Caillaux (below him), Marcel Cachin (bottom left) and Léon Blum (bottom right).

Poincaré is cutting down the tree of which they all form branches with a saw. There is a pun in the title. 'Ces discours' refers to critical speeches made by Poincaré's opponents. The comment 'quelle scie' can mean 'what a saw', or, colloquially, 'how boring'.

The implication is that Poincaré is pursuing the patriotic French course and is demolishing his critics, who are inspired by love for Germany.

5

Hope, 1924

In the middle 1920s, there were signs in many places which suggested that the world was beginning to settle down into a new and more peaceful condition after the massive upheavals of the previous decade.

That great area which had once been the Russian Empire came gradually to accept its various new systems of government. The bulk of that empire became the Soviet Union – committed, in theory at least, to the establishment of a socialist system of economic and political organization. The various anti-Bolshevik armies, whether composed of Russian citizens or of foreign interventionists, either collapsed or withdrew.

At the same time, the idea that Soviet Russia should provide the epicentre for a world revolution began to recede. The theory of world revolution still remained, with the Comintern and the various Communist Parties as its instruments; in practice, the Soviet Union gradually came to behave not very differently from other countries in its international dealings. Even the internal economy of the country seemed to become less sharply different from that of its neighbours, through the 'New Economic Policy' initiated by Lenin in the closing years of his life.

Lenin himself fell ill in 1923, and died early in the following year; thereafter, a profound struggle for the succession began, and for a very long time the Soviet Union was in no condition to intervene substantially in world affairs, while other powers, which had once sought to destroy the Soviet system, came gradually to accept it as a permanent feature of the contemporary world.

There were signs that the deep dispute among ex-belligerents over the related questions of reparations and war debts might be resolved. The French general election held in May 1924 produced a marked shift away from the *Bloc national*, in favour of various parties in the *Cartel des Gauches*, particularly the Radicals and the Socialists. Faced with this repudiation of his policies, the redoubtable Poincaré resigned in the following month. In Germany, the policy of 'passive resistance' to French occupation of the Ruhr was ended in September 1923. Two months later, the runaway inflation was brought to a sudden halt by introduction of the new Rentenmark.

An important American initiative did much to encourage a better relationship between the former belligerents. In April 1924, the American banker General Charles G. Dawes* proposed a scheme under which Germany would receive substantial loans to stabilise her currency, and would thenceforth pay reparations at an agreed annual rate.

The major European governments soon accepted the principle of the 'Dawes Plan', which looked encouraging; but it would be naïve to ignore the special circumstances – one might almost say the hypocrisy – which prompted the French and Germans in the matter. The Germans never regarded reparations in any form as other than an imposition set upon them by the victors, of which they hoped one day to be completely free. The French were far from happy with the arrangements, but were forced into them for financial reasons.

Yet the Dawes Plan was undeniably better than nothing for both of them, and at the London Conference in the following August it secured general acceptance by the European countries. There was still an element of dictation to Germany, however, in the London Conference arrangements; for the former European Allies first settled their own requirements between themselves, and only then brought Germany into the conversations. Even after acceptance of the Dawes Plan, French occupation of the Ruhr continued for a time, but it was eventually ended in the summer of the following year.

In 1925, major efforts were made to secure a more permanent reconciliation between the European powers. These efforts owed much to the wisdom and genuine collaboration of Edouard Herriot, the French Foreign Minister, and his German counterpart Gustav Stresemann. These endeavours led to the group of treaties concluded at Locarno in December of that year. One of the most important features of the Locarno arrangements was that Germany participated as an equal with the other powers and freely acknowledged the arrangements reached. Thus Locarno never acquired the opprobrium in Germany which had attached to the Versailles settlement, or even to an extent to the conclusions of the London Conference.

France and Germany acknowledged each other's frontiers, while Britain and Italy guaranteed each one against aggression from the other. Both France and Germany accepted that the Rhineland should remain, for the time being, in Allied occupation, but should eventually be demilitarized completely. France – against British advice, but with condonation from all participants at Locarno – concluded treaties of mutual assistance with Poland and Czechoslovakia. Those treaties would prove of immense importance in the late 1930s.

---

* His military title derived from the role which he played in the war as Chief of Supply for the American army in France.

Cartoon 5.1 The American plan. *San Francisco Chronicle,*
16 January 1924

THE AMERICAN PLAN

Early in 1924, the 'Dawes Plan' was put forward in the United States as
a possible way of cutting through the ill-will and confusion which had
long attended the reparations question.

In this American cartoon, General Dawes, Director of the Reparations
Finance Board, is compelling the musty, cobweb-ridden Europeans to face
'facts', to adopt 'common sense' and to practise 'cooperation'.

This American view of Europeans as antiquated fuddy-duddies, whose
quarrels bore little relation to realities of the contemporary world, is
typical of American attitudes of the period.

Cartoon 5.2 Gallic cock. *Daily Express*, London, 10 March 1924

GALLIC COCK: "What's the matter with the sun ? The more I crow the lower it gets ! " '

French Premier Raymond Poincaré crows on the dung-hill of weapons in the Ruhr. He expects to greet – perhaps even to produce – the 'sunrise' of the franc. Instead, the reverse happens.

As France became increasingly implicated in her 'direct action' policies in the Ruhr, world disapproval mounted. At the same time, France was resorting to inflationary policies, similar in kind though not in degree to those which Germany was also adopting to finance the Ruhr escapade. The combined effect of French inflation and world financial pressures was to depress the franc.

Cartoon 5.3 His Waterloo Bridge. *Star*, London, 13 May 1924

His Waterloo Bridge.

The financial consequences of Poincaré's policies probably played a considerable part in determining the results of the French elections of May 1924. Poincaré's political supporters were defeated, and in the following month Poincaré resigned office.

In this British cartoon, Poincaré, as Napoleon, is prevented from crossing his collapsing 'Waterloo Bridge' into 'Dreamland' 'by order of the French people'.

The old Waterloo Bridge in London, a structure of considerable aesthetic merit and historical interest, was in a state of disrepair about this time, and was the subject of considerable discussion among Londoners. Eventually, in the 1930s, the decision was taken to pull down the old bridge and replace it by the present structure.

Cartoon 5.4 Their kind action for the day. *Star*, London, 7 August 1924

Their Kind Action For The Day.

This cartoon was drawn just before formal acceptance of the Dawes Plan by the European governments, but at a time when that acceptance was almost certain to occur.

The Boy Scouts – Edouard Herriot of France, Ramsay MacDonald of Britain, Benito Mussolini of Italy and Hans Luther of Germany – conduct 'poor old Europe' to the safety of the 'Dawes traffic island'. Drivers of vehicles held up by the pedestrians look on with sullen expressions. The bus – one of the open-top petrol buses which were still in use in London in 1924 – carries the 'unlucky' number 13 and the destination-board for 'Ruin'.

It is striking to note that in this period Mussolini was not regarded as in any way 'beyond the pale' by the cartoonist, whose own opinions were very far indeed from 'Fascism'. The word 'Fascist' was already used in Russian as a highly pejorative term, which covered German Nazism as well as the Italian phenomenon, but it did not have a similar force in English.

Cartoon 5.5 Neofitsial'ny uchastnik londonskoi konferentsy.
Izvestiya, Moscow, 18 July 1924

НЕОФИЦИАЛЬНЫЙ УЧАСТНИК ЛОНДОНСКОЙ КОНФЕРЕНЦИИ.

Рис. Бор. Ефимова.

ЮЗ (скромно) – Надеюсь, господа, я вам не помешаю

This Soviet cartoon provides a very unfavourable view of the impact of
the United States on the European countries and the nature of the Dawes
Plan. Uncle Sam lolls at ease on a huge trunk labelled 'European debts',
and remarks casually, 'I hope, gentlemen, that I am not troubling you!'
MacDonald of Britain and Herriot of France look on in dismay. The
American trunk occupies nearly all of the conference table, and other
papers are scattered on the floor.

Cartoon 5.6 Free at last! *Star*, London, 19 August 1924

FREE AT LAST!

By contrast, this British cartoon takes a very sanguine attitude. Europe is 'free at last' after a decade of incarceration in the 'International Asylum for the Insane'. The cartoonist seems to believe that the relatively friendly international atmosphere which characterized the London Conference will persist and develop further.

Cartoon 5.7 While others talk. *Chicago Tribune,*
19 October 1924

This cartoon was drawn a couple of months after Cartoons 5.5 and 5.6, and is making a point more closely related to American domestic politics than to the international questions to which it alludes.

The American presidential and congressional elections of 1924 were approaching their climax. Calvin Coolidge had succeeded President Harding on the latter's death in August 1923, and was currently defending the presidency in the Republican interest. Charles Dawes, nominal author of the Dawes Plan, was standing for the vice-presidency as Coolidge's running-mate. The much-improved international atmosphere and the apparent effect of Dawes in bringing this about were an important campaign plank for the Republicans. The *Chicago Tribune* was supporting the Republicans, and took a very strong 'isolationist' line.

The Dawes Plan pushes a wheelbarrow-load of dollars, labelled 'Loan to Germany' along a plank from the United States in the direction of 'Rebuilding of Europe'. Anti-government agitators, probably visualized as members of the opposition Democratic Party, ignore the practical assistance which is being given to Europe, and recommend other less useful ways of helping.

One orator proposes that the United States should join the League of Nations. This harks back to the strong support for the League idea which the Democrat President Wilson had given in 1918–19. Another makes an 'appeal to alien nationalities'. In American elections, candidates often made (and still make) an appeal for support to American citizens who retain emotional links with countries from which they, or their ancestors, derived.

6

Stability, 1925–9

The later 1920s were a period of remarkable stability in Europe. There appeared good reason for thinking that the continent had settled down to a durable peace. Perhaps few people really liked the existing international arrangements, but those arrangements were seen as vastly preferable to any attempt to disrupt them through war.

In most places, the type of political system which was established in the middle of the decade seemed to be strengthening itself. In the Soviet Union, the long struggle for succession to Lenin was resolved in favour of Stalin, while his most serious rival, Trotsky, was first defeated, then disgraced and finally exiled. A sort of stability seemed to have returned. In Italy, Mussolini's Fascists were able to effect significant changes in the country's constitutional structure. There was much in Italy which democrats found deeply objectionable, but the country was still a long way from the sort of behaviour, both internally and internationally, which would later give such a pejorative sense to the name of its political system. Other European countries, notably Spain and Poland, were developing in the direction of dictatorship; but those dictatorships were also far short of the universality which the word 'totalitarianism' implies.

Throughout most of western and central Europe, a democratic pattern of government seemed well entrenched. Poincaré returned to the French premiership in 1926, and remained there for three years; but there was little scope for the policies with which he had been associated in 1923, and his Foreign Minister Briand was not the man to engage in provocative adventures. In Germany, the most significant figure was not so much President Hindenburg or the successive Chancellors, as the Foreign Minister Gustav Stresemann, who provided a continuity for his country's policy from 1923 until his death in 1929. Perhaps the climax of Stresemann's work was the acceptance of Germany in 1926 as a member of the League of Nations. This was taken as a sign both of Germany's peaceful intentions and of the willingness of others to accept her as an equal.

In Britain, the brief Labour Government of 1924 gave way to nearly five years of Conservative rule; but the Conservative Prime Minister Stanley Baldwin, like his Labour predecessor and eventual successor, Ramsay MacDonald, was seen essentially as a man of peace. Sir Austen Chamberlain, son of Joseph and half-brother of the ill-fated Neville, was one of the principal architects of Locarno, and presided over the Foreign Office for the period 1924–9.

Active preparations were made for evacuation of Allied troops from the Rhineland, which eventually took place in 1930 – nearly five years ahead of the original schedule. Slow, but active, preparations were made for a World Disarmament Conference, which was to meet in the early 1930s, and which every substantial country in the world proposed to attend.

In 1927, Briand inaugurated the idea of the formal renunciation of war as an instrument of policy. This was taken up with alacrity by various European countries and then by the United States, whose Secretary of State Frank B. Kellogg cooperated to produce in August 1928 the agreement to that effect which became known as the Kellogg, or sometimes as the Kellogg–Briand, Pact. Not the least encouraging feature of that arrangement was that sixty-five nations, including Germany, the United States and the Soviet Union, subscribed to its terms. There was surely some poignancy in the fact that this declaration could be made when the great warrior Hindenburg was President of Germany and the fire-eating Poincaré head of the French government.

The vexed question of German reparations seemed to be moving towards a permanent solution. A committee headed by the American businessman Owen D. Young produced a scheme which reduced the old figure substantially, and required Germany to pay annuities until 1988. The Germans and others affected all accepted the Young Plan.

Around the end of the decade, a series of events took place which in various ways set the scene for the baleful events of the 1930s. In 1929 Italy became, in form as well as in reality, a one-party state. In the same year, Stalin made hesitant beginnings to the forced collectivization of Soviet agriculture, which was to cost the lives of many millions of his country's citizens. The 'great depression' and its consequences will be considered in later chapters.

Cartoon 6.1 Cartoon from *Becco Giallo*, Rome, reprinted in *L'Europe Nouvelle*, Paris, 11 April 1925

M. HERRIOT: Qu'en pensez-vous?
M. CAILLAUX: Avant tout, il faut changer la malade de lit.
(Extrait de *Becco Giallo*, de Rome.)

Edouard Herriot, who combined the portfolios of Premier and Foreign Minister, and Joseph Caillaux, the newly appointed Minister of Finance, are doctors attending the bloated patient Marianne. Her bed is made of weapons of war; on the wall are portraits of Millerand (President 1920–4), Clemenceau and Marshal Foch – all of them political personalities who had been associated with assertive and militaristic policies.

Caillaux had long been a highly controversial figure in French politics. He had opposed French participation in the First World War, and was eventually imprisoned for his stand on the matter. He was a trenchant critic of Versailles, and noted for advanced views on taxation questions. He was, inevitably, a strong opponent of high military expenditure.

Herriot asks Caillaux what he thinks of Marianne's case. The answer is that, first and foremost, the patient needs a change of bed – that is, that France must adopt less militaristic policies.

Cartoon 6.2 And now the next step! *Star*, London, 1 December 1925

In the mid-1920s, there was considerable optimism in Europe. The Locarno agreements, concluded towards the end of 1925, were generally welcomed as important moves towards general peace.

In this British cartoon, Europa has already advanced from the Dawes Plan (1924) to the Locarno Treaties, and is now prepared for the more difficult, but not impossible, next step, disarmament. The governments represented at Locarno accepted the idea that they would now work out plans for general disarmament, in preparation for a World Disarmament Conference which would be held at an unspecified date.

Cartoon 6.3 Bessil'ny maestro. *Pravda*, Moscow,
3 December 1925

Бессильный маэстро.

Рис. МАЙНЕЛЯ.

This Soviet cartoon, 'Powerless maestro', takes a very different view of Locarno. The despairing British chess-master, Foreign Secretary Sir Austen Chamberlain, sets his pawns – Poland, Czechoslovakia, France and Germany – against the much more impressive piece 'USSR', whose proletarian face regards his opponents with visible contempt.

The likenesses on the pawns are not very good. The head of the piece Poland seems to be that of Pilsudski. He was not at that time in control of the Polish government, but had been the military leader in the war of independence a few years earlier. The piece Czechoslovakia apparently carries the head of Foreign Minister Eduard Beneš, although the representation is particularly poor. France is headed by Foreign Minister Briand, and Germany by Foreign Minister Stresemann, who are more recognizable.

The implication is that the Locarno agreements were designed primarily to damage the Soviet Union, but that they were bound to fail. The first part of that judgement, at least, seems to be erroneous. There is little, if any, evidence that European governments of the mid-1920s were either plotting to destroy the Soviet Union, or particularly fearful of its likely effects upon their own countries in the foreseeable future. Chamberlain

91

was much more concerned to resolve disputes between France and Germany.

As for the roles of Czechoslovakia and Poland, the British Foreign Office showed no enthusiasm whatever for the eastern alliances which so interested the French. Those alliances, indeed, were designed essentially to protect Germany's neighbours against a German military recrudescence, not with reference to the Soviet Union.

It is important, however, to recall that memories of the Russian civil war and of the intervention of Allied forces both before and after the 1918 Armistice were still vivid. Soviet suspicion was understandable, but it was no doubt nurtured by the country's government.

This is another Soviet cartoon taking a cynical view of Locarno. Leading statesmen are seen as 'Types from the world stage'.

President Coolidge, of the United States, is the 'beneficent father', and carries the placard 'We give credit at a good percentage'. This refers to America's role as the general international creditor. Briand of France is the 'tragedian', carrying a paper labelled 'French bankruptcy' – an allusion to the frequent French complaints about their country's economic difficulties. Mussolini of Italy is the 'first lover' – a reference, perhaps, to his flamboyant personality, and perhaps to his many sexual adventures. On his shirt is the word 'Fascism' and a swastika. The latter was surely inappropriate at that date, for Mussolini was bitterly opposed to the Nazis, who seemed to challenge Italian interests in the South Tyrol and elsewhere. Beneš of Czechoslovakia is the 'comic', and carries the bill 'I still haven't recognized the USSR'. President Hindenburg of Germany, represented as a senile character, is the 'dramatic old woman', carrying the paper 'peace of Versailles', which refers to the constant German grievance. Finally, Sir Austen Chamberlain of Britain is 'stage manager', and carries the script of the 'Locarno performance'.

Cartoon 6.4 Tipy mirovoi stseny. *Pravda*, Moscow,
18 November 1925

Cartoon 6.5 'Say it with nails'. *Evening Standard*, London, 22 April 1925

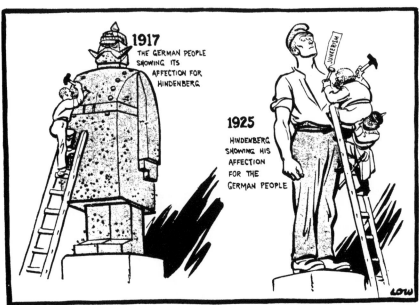

" SAY IT WITH NAILS ! "

This British cartoon comments bitterly on the election of Paul von Hindenburg as German President in 1925, following the death of Ebert.

Hindenburg had been the most charismatic German military leader in the war. At one point, a huge wooden statue of the Field Marshal was erected in Berlin, and people making donations to war charities were permitted to drive nails into it.

In this cartoon, Hindenburg, supported by a German officer wearing the familiar spiked helmet, is hammering the nail 'Junkerism' into the heart of the new Germany, which wears the Phrygian cap of liberty. The Junkers were German, and particularly Prussian, landowners, whose economic preponderance and military ethos were two of the most widely deplored features of pre-war Germany.

Cartoon 6.6 Scène de ménage. *Kladderadatsch*, Berlin, copied in *L'Europe Nouvelle*, Paris, 20 November 1926

Scène de ménage

Le « père » Poincaré au « petit » Aristide Briand :
Au lieu de couper des branches de palmier, vous
feriez mieux de retrouver le franc perdu, polisson !
(Extrait du *Kladderadatsch*, de Berlin.)

This German cartoon comments on the different attitudes of French Premier Poincaré and his Foreign Minister Briand.

Poincaré, the father, reprimands his son Briand in the presence of mother Marianne: 'Instead of cutting palm branches, you would have done better to recover the lost franc, you fool!' In Poincaré's view, it is suggested, Briand should have given more attention to France's immediate economic interests, and not to the task of securing a lasting peace with Germany.

Cartoon 6.7 Perelivanie iz pustovo v porozhnee. *Izvestiya*, Moscow, 2 March 1928

Переливание из пустого в порожнее.

Гпо. Бор. Ефимов.

БРИАН И КЕЛЛОГ ПЕРЕГОВАРИВАЮТСЯ О «ВЕЧНОМ МИРЕ» И ЗАПРЕ-ЩЕНИИ ВОЙНЫ.

'Decanting from emptiness to emptiness' is a deeply cynical Soviet cartoon about the 'Kellogg–Briand Pact' of 1928. The idea, deriving from French Foreign Minister Aristide Briand (on the left in the cartoon) and American Secretary of State Frank B. Kellogg, was that nations should make declarations formally outlawing war. At the time, the idea was widely supported, and many countries adhered.

The wording at the bottom of the cartoon is to the effect that the two statesmen have been discussing the preservation of peace or avoidance of war. The implication is that neither has anything useful in his mind to contribute on the subject.

Nevertheless, the Soviet Union did eventually adhere to the Kellogg–Briand Pact.

Cartoon 6.8 L'évacuation de la Rhénanie. *Kladderadatsch,* Berlin, copied in *L'Europe Nouvelle,* Paris, 21 July 1928

La France disait avant les élections allemandes : « Tant que l'Allemagne gardera son gouvernement conservateur actuel et méditera une revanche, il ne peut être question ni de désarmement, ni de l'évacuation de !a Rhénanie. »

La France dit, après les élections allemandes de mai 1928 : « Comment protéger mon pauvre pays contre cette vague de bolchevisme sanguinaire qui vient d'Allemagne ? Il n'est vraiment plus possible, maintenant, de parler de désarmement ni de l'évacuation de la Rhénanie. »

(Extrait du *Kladderadatsch,* de Berlin.)

This German cartoon suggests that there is a fundamental inconsistency, even hypocrisy, in French attitudes to the questions of disarmament and military evacuation of the Rhineland.

Marianne – France – wears military decorations and a huge sword, a reference to the French army, which was probably the strongest in Europe. Before the German elections of 1928, Marianne points to a picture of Prime Minister Wilhelm Marx, leader of the Catholic *Zentrum,* and protests, 'While Germany preserves its present Conservative Government and contemplates revenge, there can be no question either of disarmament or of evacuation of the Rhineland.'

But the 1928 elections produced a substantial swing towards the political 'left', and a change of Prime Minister. After the elections, Marianne points to a portrait of Marx's Social Democratic successor Hermann Müller, and protests, 'How can my poor country be protected from this wave of bloody Bolshevism which is coming from Germany? It is no longer possible now to speak either of disarmament or of evacuation of the Rhineland.' Whatever the politics of Germany might be, France would find some excuse for not disarming, and for holding on to the Rhineland.

In the event, France did soon decide to evacuate the Rhineland, and her troops finally left the area in the middle of 1930.

Cartoon 6.9 Le nouvel édifice des réparations.
Kladderadatsch, Berlin, copied in *L'Europe Nouvelle*, Paris,
15 December 1928

Le nouvel édifice des réparations

'Est-ce le temple de la reconciliation ou un etab-
lissement pénitentiaire?'
(Extrait du *Kladderadatsch*, de Berlin.)

This German cartoon refers to the renewed discussions about reparations
and war debts which eventually led to the 'Young Plan', which superseded
the earlier 'Dawes Plan' in 1929. 'Michel', who peers through the fence
of the building site, is a character often used by German cartoonists to
personify Germany, rather as Britain was often personified by John Bull,
or the United States by Uncle Sam. The title of the edifice in process of
construction is 'New reparations building', and there is a notice underneath reading 'No unauthorized persons admitted'.

Behind the 'fence', discussions are taking place between Poincaré of
France and Parker Gilbert of the United States on the reparations question.
Michel speculates whether the building they are constructing is to be a
temple of reconciliation or a penal compound for convicts. In either event,
he is being firmly excluded from the discussions.

The Young Plan was set out in June 1929 and later accepted by
Germany. A first payment was made by Germany in the following year,
but almost immediately the Great Depression became so intense that
further payment was suspended. The Plan was later formally repudiated
by Hitler.

Cartoon 6.10 Récréation fasciste. *Arbeiter Zeitung*, Vienna, copied in *L'Europe Nouvelle*, 11 December 1925

Récréation fasciste

Mussolini chatouille avec une plume de paon
le dieu de la guerre endormi.
(Extrait de l'*Arbeiter Zeitung*, de Vienne.)

Mussolini's role in world politics varied considerably during the later 1920s. At times he appeared as a constructive world statesman, neither more nor less aggressively militarist than most of his contemporaries. Italy, which had seized much territory from Austro-Hungary after the First World War, had good reason to fear any renewal of the conflict. At other times, however, Mussolini made speeches, perhaps intended primarily for domestic consumption, which glorified war and violence.

The Austrian cartoonist probably had one of the latter occasions in mind when he drew the cartoon 'Mussolini tickles with a peacock feather the sleeping god of war'. The dictator wears the Fascist black shirt, and holds the *fasces*, an ancient Roman symbol adopted by Fascist Italy.

Cartoon 6.11 König und Kirchenstaat. *Simplicissimus*, Munich, 1929

König und Kirchenstaat   (Th. Th. Heine)

„Bittschön, großer Mussolini, gib mir auch ein Fleckchen italienischer Erde, wo ich herrschen darf."

In this cartoon of 1929, King Victor Emmanuel III of Italy pleads with the dictator, 'I beg you, great Mussolini, to give me, to give me too, a corner of Italian territory where I can govern.'

Italy had just reached a concordat with the Papacy, to the effect that Vatican City should become a completely independent sovereign state, thus reviving in microcosm the Papal States over which the Pope had exercised the powers of a temporal sovereign before they were seized by the kingdom of Italy in 1870. Mussolini is extracting an episcopal crozier from the *fasces* to give to the Pope. The dome of St Peter's Cathedral is seen in the background. The King, whose once considerable powers had been seriously eroded by Mussolini, seeks some kind of compensation for his loss of authority similar to that which has been granted to the Pope.

100

Cartoon 6.12 La réforme électorale italienne. *Becco Giallo*, Rome, copied in *L'Europe Nouvelle*, Paris, 16 March 1929

La réforme électorale italienne

L'électeur, voyant affichée a la porte de la salle de vote l'interdiction de voter contre les candidats [officiels] demande : « Pardon, où irai-je voter contre ? » « En face, au cimetière », lui répond le fonctionnaire du bureau.

Extrait de *Becco Giallo*.)

The text reads, 'The voter, seeing a notice posted on the door of the polling booth forbidding people to vote against the [official] candidates, asks, "Excuse me, where do I go to vote against?" "Opposite, to the cemetery", the polling officer tells him.'

This cartoon refers to the various changes which were introduced in Italy which made the country a one-party state. 'Elections' were still held, but there were few opportunities for critics to vote against the Fascists. At the time when the cartoon was drawn, there had been political murders conducted in Italy by the Fascists, and it alludes obliquely to those crimes.

Cartoon 6.13 Le nouveau cabinet polonais. *Le Canard Enchaîné*, Paris, 17 April 1928

LE NOUVEAU CABINET POLONAIS TIENT SA PREMIERE SEANCE

Although in general the late 1920s were a period of considerable international reconciliation, there remained a number of causes for concern. This cartoon and the next two allude to three of them.

In the French cartoon of 1928, 'The new Polish Cabinet holds its first meeting', Marshal Pilsudski greets what is not an ordinary civilian Cabinet but, in effect, a group of military leaders. Parliamentary democracy was never very successful in Poland, and in 1926 was brought to an end by a military *putsch* by Marshal Pilsudski. Two years later the country became in some respects a military dictatorship.

Poland had recently been engaged in a serious territorial dispute with her neighbour Lithuania. This dispute had been resolved through the League of Nations, but there was still a good deal of anti-Polish feeling in many places.

Cartoon 6.14 Grande-Bretagne et Egypte. *Guerin Meschino*, Milan, copied in *L'Europe Nouvelle*, Paris, 2 June 1928

Grande-Bretagne et Egypte

Les nations : « Dites-nous, M. John Bull, est-ce là la théorie du désarmement ?
— Non, seulement la pratique. »
(Extrait du *Guerin Meschino*, de Milan.)

This Italian cartoon alludes to the persistence of 'old style' British imperialism. Egypt had been under strong British influence since the 1880s. For a brief period, it ranked as a British Protectorate. That state of affairs had ended, but British domination persisted.

In March 1928, a treaty was negotiated between the British Foreign Secretary and the Egyptian Premier, which was to give Britain enormous authority in Egypt. The proposed treaty was rejected by the Egyptian government. A bill was introduced into the Egyptian Parliament which was considered to reduce the protection given to foreigners in Egypt. Eventually a British ultimatum was sent to Egypt, and British warships were ordered to proceed there. The Egyptian government then capitulated, and the warships were withdrawn.

Britain's overweening behaviour was widely resented in other countries. Preparation for the future World Disarmament Conference was still in progress, and the cartoon alludes to this matter. The European nations address Britain, 'Tell us, Mr John Bull, is that the theory of disarmament?' To that question John Bull replies, 'No, only the practice.'

Cartoon 6.15 Those disquieting sounds. *Chicago Tribune*, 29 October 1929

This American cartoon refers to another cause of international concern in the late 1920s. The turkey 'World Peace' is caged under 'protection of the Kellogg Treaty' – that is, the treaty renouncing war which had recently been signed by many countries, including Italy and the Soviet Union. His food is 'disarmament'.

The unfortunate bird listens with obvious concern to the 'disquieting sounds' of an axe and a knife being ground on the wheels 'Italy' and 'Russia'. Mussolini had just made a very bellicose speech, glorying in Italy's military strength and referring to 'great battles' which his Fascists might be called upon to fight in the future. At almost the same moment, a Soviet diplomat in Paris, who had just escaped from his embassy in dramatic circumstances, published articles in the *Daily Telegraph* alluding to plans of the Soviet leaders in 1924 to stir up disruption in Britain and make it the centre of world revolution.

Thus the turkey had considerable cause to doubt whether all nations were sincere in their protestations of peaceful intent.

7

The Great Depression begins, 1929–31

From the end of the First World War, the United States had been the 'universal creditor' to whom all the ex-belligerents owed money, and whose finances and economy were far stronger than any in Europe. The European ex-belligerents, and other countries too, constantly complained about this state of affairs. In America, however, a great many people – most of them people of quite modest means – were eagerly investing in the apparently limitless prosperity of their economy.

Suddenly, in October 1929, the boom was shattered by the 'Wall Street crash'. Many people were ruined. The general optimism collapsed. By the end of the year the United States was in serious recession, with rising unemployment.

Early in 1930, the Great Depression began to affect Europe, and most particularly countries like Britain and Germany which had highly-developed industrial economies. In Britain, where unemployment had been a major problem for nearly a decade, the situation rapidly deteriorated, and in the course of 1930 the unemployment figures nearly doubled. In Germany, where unemployment was linked with poverty of a kind more extreme than in Britain, and where the proportion of unemployed was even greater, the very fabric of society began to crumble.

By a strange coincidence, these troubles of the 'capitalist' world were taking place at the same moment as the more or less isolated Soviet Union was experiencing disruptions on an even more massive scale. The forced collectivization of Soviet agriculture led to an enormous amount of starvation, and deaths which must be numbered in many millions. Stalin purchased immunity from revolution at the price of the most all-pervasive tyranny the world had yet seen.

Throughout the world, economic systems became increasingly unstable. Producers faced with contracting domestic markets tried to persuade their governments to apply tariffs and other devices to exclude foreign competition. The overall effect was to exaggerate the Depression, and also to embitter the peoples of all countries against their neighbours.

In the United States elections of November 1928, the victorious Republicans had promised a revision of the tariff system. This revision was carried out in the first half of 1930, by which time the Depression was hanging over the country. The 'Smoot–Hawley tariffs' which eventually emerged were a good deal higher than had been anticipated, and this inevitably set off a chain-reaction elsewhere in favour of national tariffs.

In Britain, the traditional policy of free trade had been somewhat eroded during the war and its aftermath, but was still retained in its essentials throughout the 1920s. In the course of 1930, great pressure was set up in favour of tariffs, although for a time there was considerable argument among protectionists as to what form these tariffs should take. Tariffs were eventually imposed in 1932, in circumstances which will be considered later. Inevitably, these developments in Britain and the United States gave substance to the arguments of protectionists in other countries, and led to a general spate of tariffs.

The one significant attempt to counter the Depression by actually reducing tariffs ran into trouble of a different kind. In March 1931, the German and Austrian governments agreed to a customs union (*Zollverein*) between the two countries. There was much argument whether or not this arrangement was permissible under international law; but, legal or not, the French set out to wreck it. As a result, the great Austrian bank Kreditanstalt was soon in serious difficulties. The terms on which the French offered to rescue the bank were onerous, and another serious cause of international hostility had arisen.

Cartoon 7.1 En marge de la conférence des experts. *Guerin Meschino*, Milan, copied in *L'Europe Nouvelle*, Paris, 25 May 1929

En marge de la Conférence des experts

Explication du problème des dettes interalliées à l'usage des citoyens européens.

(Extrait du *Guerin Meschino*, de Milan.)

These three cartoons, from different countries which often had antagonistic interests, express a common resentment against American economic ascendancy. All of them were drawn in the late 1920s, but before the 'Wall Street crash' took place in October 1929.

The Italian cartoon proposes an 'explanation of the problem of inter-Allied debts for the convenience of citizens of Europe'. The European countries pour money into the right-hand vessel, which bears the features of John Bull. That money merely passes through John Bull into Uncle Sam, the ultimate recipient of reparations and war debts.

The second cartoon, 'The regulation of war debts', derives from Australia, and makes a strong moral point. Uncle Sam complains to Justice that he has purchased crutches for the various European war-wounded – in other words, he has advanced financial assistance to European countries – and they now do not wish to pay him. Justice retorts, 'But have they not been wounded in fighting for you?'

Cartoon 7.2 Le règlement des dettes de guerre. *Bulletin*, Sydney, 28 July 1928, copied in *L'Europe Nouvelle*, Paris, 28 July 1928

Le règlement des dettes de guerre

L'ONCLE SAM : « Mais, dites donc, c'est moi qui'ai acheté pour eux leurs béquilles, et ils ne veulent pas me les payer. »

LA JUSTICE : « Mais n'ont-ils pas été blessés en combattant pour vous ? »

[Allusion à la recrudescence d'agitation aux Etats-Unis en faveur de l'annulation des dettes de guerre.]

(Extrait du *Bulletin*, de Sydney.)

Cartoon 7.3 Die vereinigten Staaten von Europa.
Simplicissimus, Munich, 5 August 1929

DIE
VEREINIGTEN STAATEN
VON EUROPA

The third cartoon, 'The United States of Europe', alludes to the proposal from French Foreign Minister Briand that the European countries should work towards political union. The cartoon suggests that the European states are already united economically: they constitute a slave gang which is carrying a large bag of dollars for the benefit of Uncle Sam.

Cartoon 7.4 Stock market fever chart. *Washington Post,*
21 October 1929

Stock Market Fever Chart.   — Detroit News.

The 'Wall Street crash' of October 1929 was extremely abrupt. This
cartoon from the *Washington Post* emphasizes both its sudden character
and its effect on small investors.

In the preceding period, a great many people of very modest means
had been speculating in stocks and shares, on the tacit assumption that
the boom condition would continue indefinitely. Many had put their life
savings in securities whose value collapsed within hours. The misery was
great; but it was not immediately obvious that the slump was to have a
profound long-term effect on the economy of the United States and of
most other countries as well.

Cartoon 7.5 Leaves are scattered, but the tree is unchanged.
San Francisco Chronicle, 30 October 1929.

Leaves Are Scattered but Tree Is Unchanged

Cartoons 7.5 and 7.6 both appeared within a few days of the 'Wall Street crash' in newspapers which had tended to support the Republican Administration of President Hoover, but they express rather different views of the likely long-term effects of the 'crash'.

The *San Francisco Chronicle* suggests that the 'crash' was a brief phenomenon. The leaves have fallen; easy profits have vanished, and the investing public has been driven before the gale; but the tree, 'American industry', is as sound as ever, and will no doubt soon recover.

111

Cartoon 7.6 An untrustworthy machine. *Chicago Tribune,* 22 October 1929

The *Chicago Tribune* is less certain. The cartoon is remarkable as a very early reference to television, which had been invented about four years earlier. The stock investor is disturbed when the 'beautiful picture' of a fat and confident 'American business' suddenly becomes distorted. The reader must have asked whether it was the picture or the subject which had suddenly changed, and whether it was really the machine which had suddenly become 'untrustworthy'.

Cartoon 7.7 Wicked for business to protect itself! *San Francisco Chronicle*, 28 October 1929

This cartoon appeared at the very beginning of the Depression, long before people had decided that it was likely to be a protracted affair, or its worst effects had begun to be felt.

As has been noted, the question of revising, and probably increasing, American tariffs had played a part in the Republican campaign for the elections of November 1928. The cartoon expresses sympathy with Republican views on the matter. It is argued that, if labour and the agricultural interest can both obtain special favours from the government by lobbying Congress, then 'business' has a similar claim, and special favours may legitimately be sought from Congress to deal with problems of manufacturing industry. The factory in the background is closed; the implication seems to be that some kind of government assistance, perhaps by way of tariffs against foreign competition, would assist 'business' to overcome its difficulties.

Cartoon 7.8 Tarif douanier américain. *Louisville Courier-Journal,* copied in *L'Europe Nouvelle,* 10 May 1930

Tarif douanier américain

C'est le consommateur américain qui fera les frais des modifications apportées par le Sénat de Washington à la loi douanière, en faisant hausser le prix de la vie.

(Extrait du *Courier-Journal* de Louisville.)

This cartoon presents a different view of the tariff question. In the spring of 1930, Congress was giving active consideration to the idea of increasing tariffs substantially. The cartoonist points out that tariff increases will necessarily involve added costs, which will have to be paid by the American consumer.

Cartoon 7.9 Some frail. *Evening Standard*, London,
21 June 1930

SOME FRAIL.

The title appears to derive from Shelley's poem 'To Wordsworth', which contains a reference to 'some frail bark in winter's midnight roar'.

The question of increased American tariffs was currently before Senate, which was preparing to 'lower away' a 'record tariff'. Senate is being encouraged by 'interests'. One of the most striking features of the United States tariff debate was the 'log-rolling' process by which different interest groups joined forces to secure tariffs for their various products.

The 'frail bark' into which the corpulent 'record tariff' is being lowered is piloted by the 'U.S. exporter', who views the process with alarm. A nation can only pay for its imports by its exports; thus, a policy designed to reduce American imports through tariffs will necessarily damage American exports. American 'business' does not all have the same interest; a policy which is beneficial for some sections will prove disastrous for others.

Cartoon 7.10 Les dangers du protectionnisme. *New York Telegram*, copied in *L'Europe Nouvelle*, Paris, 30 August 1930

Les dangers du protectionnisme [1].

Diable, on dirait qu'il devient un peu trop gros !
(Extrait du *New-York Telegram.*)

In the end, 'log-rolling' by interested parties resulted in American tariffs (the 'Smoot–Hawley tariffs') considerably higher than even the protectionists had originally envisaged. In this cartoon, as the enormous tariff pig is dragged out of Congress, two Congressmen meditate 'Maybe we let it get too big'.

Some historians have argued that the Smoot–Hawley tariffs were not really as enormous as world opinion suggested. Whether this is correct or not, the world certainly saw those tariffs as a huge American lunge in the direction of protection, and they were followed rapidly by a general move towards protectionism elsewhere. World trade clogged up, the Depression deepened, and in some places desperate people began to contemplate breaking through tariff barriers by force. As the saying went, 'If goods cannot cross international frontiers, armies will.'

Cartoon 7.11 Dépression américaine. *Observer*, Charlotte, North Carolina, copied by *L'Europe Nouvelle*, Paris, 6 December 1930

Dépression américaine

La main-d'œuvre inutilisée et le capital sans emploi
(ensemble) : « Si seulement je trouvais à m'occuper ! »

(Extrait de l'*Observer*, de Charlotte, U. S. A.)

Inevitably, the Smoot–Hawley tariffs did not relieve the Depression, even for the United States which was imposing them, but made that Depression worse.

This American cartoon reflects on the irony of the situation. 'Idle labor' – the unemployed workers – and 'Idle money' – under-used capital – both make the same dismal comment, 'If only I could find something to do!' The unemployed worker wants a job; the potential investor wants to find a remunerative investment for his money. The strong implication is that some kind of policy is urgently required which will bring those complementary needs together for mutual benefit.

Cartoon 7.12 Le capitalisme devant le chômage. *Za Indystrializatsiou*, Moscow, copied by *L'Europe Nouvelle*, Paris, 30 May 1931

Le capitalisme devant le chômage.
(Extrait de *Za indoustrializatsiou*, de Moscou.)

The scale of unemployment mounted rapidly. In this Soviet cartoon 'capitalism confronting unemployment', the diminutive figure representing capitalism is confonted by thirty million unemployed – a number evidently based on world-wide figures.

The cartoonist is apparently suggesting that these appalling unemployment figures represented the 'crisis of capitalism' which would lead to the final destruction of the whole system.

This cartoon really puts Runciman, the customs official, in a false position, for he certainly took no pleasure in what he was doing, but he probably reflected that it was better that he should be in charge of the measure than that it should be handled by an avowed protectionist.

Cartoon 8.10 Heroic deeds from history – No. 1. *Evening Standard*, London, 28 January 1932

After the *Abnormal Importations Act* was passed, the National Government set to work to devise a more permanent system of tariffs. Free traders in the government – the 'official' Liberals, headed by Samuel, and also Snowden from the National Labour Party – deeply opposed the idea, and were poised to resign. Then an 'agreement to differ' was devised, by which they remained free to speak and vote against the government's tariff proposals, and yet remained within the government.

Cartoon 8.10 (see page 140) is a cynical comment on the 'agreement to differ', explained by the inset at the top left. Leonidas and his Spartan hoplites at Thermopylae (480 BC) are, respectively, Sir Herbert Samuel, Sir Archibald Sinclair, Sir Donald Maclean and Philip – who had recently become Viscount – Snowden. They knew that the 'tariff hosts' were certain to proceed along the pass – but, technically, they had not abandoned it to the enemy.

The free trade ministers won little credit, and no long-term benefit, from accepting the 'agreement to differ'. Their free trade followers began to doubt their leadership, and before the year was out they had all left the National Government.

How far the British people swung from a positively free trade stance in the 1920s to a positive support for tariffs in the early 1930s is a matter of speculation. Throughout the whole period, there were substantial numbers of convinced free traders and convinced protectionists; but the issue was decided by people not firmly committed to either side. In the 1920s, they had tended to support free trade as the familiar 'status quo'; but, under impact of the Depression the people of Britain, like the people of Germany, cast around for a change. The Germans finished up with Hitler; the British finished up with protection. When most members of the National Government came out in favour of protection, most of the general public was prepared to go with them, without any deep conviction either way.

Neville Chamberlain, who was Chancellor of the Exchequer from November 1931 until he became Prime Minister in May 1937, played a critical part in the abandonment of free trade. Son of the redoubtable Joseph

Cartoon 7.14 The gentle hand. *Sunday Mercury,*
Birmingham, Alabama, copied by *Chicago Tribune,*
14 March 1930

In the American cartoon, the practical effect of this policy is seen in the
issue of enormous numbers of death warrants. The liquidation of the
kulaks produced effects far beyond the kulak class – and, indeed, beyond
the ranks of opponents of Communist policy. Peasants who may certainly
be numbered in millions, and perhaps in tens of millions, died through
the persecution and famine which resulted from this policy.

In the German cartoon, 'Death sentence in Soviet Russia', the old
woman mourns the death of some of the victims, 'But they were also
Russians, brother, people like us!' The man replies, 'But their politics,
Little Mother, their politics were different.'

Cartoon 7.15 Todesurteile in Sowjetrussland. *Simplicissimus*, Munich, 18 November 1929

„Es waren doch Russen, Brüder, Menschen wie wir." — „Ja, aber die Politik, Mütterchen, die Politik war anders!"

Cartoon 7.16 Plan quinquennal. *Izvestiya*, Moscow, copied by *L'Europe Nouvelle*, Paris, 7 March 1931

Plan quinquennal

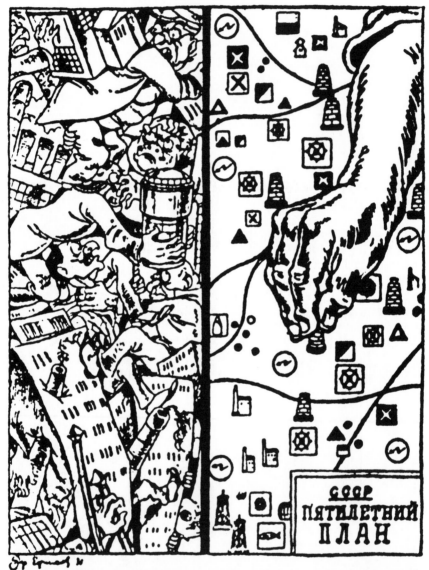

D'un côté le désordre et les rivalités des Etats capitalistes, de l'autre le jeu raisonné du communisme qui joue avec les pièces du Plan quinquennal sur l'échiquier russe.

(Extrait des *Izvestia*, de Moscou.)

The liquidation of the kulaks was but part of a much wider Soviet design, the first 'Five-Year Plan', which commenced in 1928, and was designed to restructure and modernize the whole Soviet economy.

In this Soviet cartoon, the contrast is drawn between the rivalry and disorders of capitalist states and the orderly development which was supposed to accompany the Five-Year Plan.

In this period of economic misery, many people in the 'capitalist' countries came to consider that Communism would in some way solve their own problems. They were disposed to think that the appalling horrors which were being reported from the Soviet Union were a gross exaggeration, or even a tissue of lies and calumnies. As the 1930s developed, polarization between people who saw only good in the Soviet system and those who saw in it nothing but evil, and a profound threat to all other societies became stronger and stronger.

8

The Great Depression and British politics, 1929–32

The Great Depression exerted an effect on British politics which is important not only from a national but from a world point of view. It changed British party relationships dramatically, and set up a pattern which was to continue in essentials right up to the spring of 1940. The government which came into being as a result of the Great Depression was to pursue both domestic and foreign policies which had an enormous impact on other countries in many ways.

In the late spring of 1929, before the Great Depression commenced, a general election was held in Britain. This resulted in the Labour Party forming its second government, and becoming, for the first time, the largest single party in the House of Commons, although (such are the vagaries of the British electoral system!) they received rather fewer votes than the Conservatives whom they displaced. The Liberals, who by this time were for all practical purposes led by Lloyd George, received just under sixty seats, but these were sufficient to give them the 'balance of power' and enable them, if they so chose, to drive the government from office.

Ramsay MacDonald, the new Prime Minister, had been in office for only a few months when the Wall Street crash hit the United States. At first Britain was not much affected, but early in 1930 the Great Depression crossed the Atlantic. Throughout that year and the first half of 1931, all visible signs of economic disaster, and most particularly unemployment, increased rapidly.

All parties were profoundly shaken by these events. The Labour Government came under increasing criticism from its own erstwhile supporters, who attacked from markedly different angles. Some pressed for much more socialistic policies; others considered that the government should follow policies which today we would probably call Keynesian.

The Conservative opposition encountered trouble of a different kind. The Conservatives had traditionally been the protectionist party, although they still included a few free traders within their ranks. Yet even protectionists could not forget that, on the last two occasions when Conservatives had sought to pursue an active protectionist policy, the result had been political disaster. Should they now again advocate protectionism, and invite a further rebuff? Furthermore, there was wide disagreement

124

among the protectionists themselves. As the Americans were finding, protectionist policies which are designed to benefit one industry may prove disastrous for others. The 'press lords' who controlled important Conservative newspapers veered toward a rather egregious protectionism of their own, with a strong imperial flavour.

The Conservatives were also encountering trouble of a different kind, not directly related to the tariff controversy. The Labour Government, on the prompting of the Viceroy of India, Lord Irwin (who later became even more famous as Viscount Halifax), gave its support to a policy designed to give India eventual 'dominion status', similar to that enjoyed by Canada and Australia. The Conservative leadership mostly inclined to the same view, but a number of their backbenchers, headed by Winston Churchill, dissented noisily. Thus it happened that Churchill, who had been Chancellor of the Exchequer in the Conservative Government of 1924–9, found himself profoundly at loggerheads with Stanley Baldwin and most other leaders of his party, and was driven into the political wilderness.

The Liberals were also deeply divided. As time went on, two different currents of opinion appeared. One section, headed by Lloyd George, seemed to believe that some kind of *rapprochement* was possible between the government and the Liberals, by which Liberal policies, particularly in relation to unemployment, would be pursued, and perhaps some Liberals would actually enter the government. Another section, whose most famous member was Sir John Simon, decided that no useful policies could be expected from the government, and were contemplating cooperation with the Conservatives to turn it out.

The final crisis of the Labour Government arose in a curious way. The system of unemployment insurance was based on a contributory scheme, to which employees, employers and the government all made payments. By early 1931, there was evidence that the whole scheme was in serious trouble, for the effect of high unemployment was to increase claims on the fund and to diminish the contributions received. A committee was set up, headed by Sir George May, a leading figure in the world of insurance, to report on the matter.

The May Committee's report was published at the end of July 1931. Parliament had just risen for the summer recess, and therefore the next stages of the crisis occurred at a time when MPs were not sitting, and many important people were out of the country on holiday. By a remarkable coincidence, Lloyd George had suddenly fallen dangerously ill, and for several months to come his health was not fully restored.

The May Committee report indicated that the unemployment fund was indeed seriously overdrawn, and made a number of proposals for dealing with the situation. It is important to remember that few people of any political persuasion had much doubt at the time about the reality of the crisis, or the importance of balanced budgets. Recollection of German inflation eight years earlier stirred intense fears among a large section of the public that all kinds of savings might soon become virtually worthless.

Although the need for economy was agreed, there was no corresponding agreement as to what the economy measures should be. Any proposal was bound to run against protests from people who considered that the sacrifices demanded from them were not commensurate with those required from others. The government struggled with possible economies, but it soon became apparent that there was no way in which they could devise proposals adequate to meet the situation which would also secure adequate support from the Labour Party and also from Parliament as a whole.

Nor was there much prospect of the situation being resolved by the Labour Government leaving office and being replaced by the Conservatives. The Conservatives also had no prospect of devising proposals which could be pushed through that Parliament, while, if they assumed office and promptly called a general election, the campaign itself would be so protracted that – whatever the ultimate upshot – the pound could easily collapse before it was over.

Many people began to think of some kind of coalition. The word 'coalition' had unpleasant connotations for many people in all parties, and the term 'National Government' was generally used by people who saw a possible solution on those lines. The end came suddenly. On 24 August 1931, the existing ministry resigned, and Ramsay MacDonald constituted a new National Government, with himself still Prime Minister.

At the very beginning, the National government seemed to be the closest possible approach to the genuine 'National Government' which the visionaries had suggested. In a Cabinet of ten, there were four Labour, four Conservative and two Liberal members. All agreed that the government was constituted merely to handle the immediate crisis, while, as soon as that crisis was over, the parties should resume their independence, and a new general election should be held.

Almost at once, the Labour Party repudiated its own leaders. Those leaders, however, saw no reason to withdraw from the government. The new government soon produced economy proposals. It was necessary to recall Parliament to give them legislative effect. The Conservatives, the Liberals and the Labour members of the National Government voted one way, and the bulk of the Labour Party voted the other; but the majority in favour of the proposals was adequate.

Soon pressure was mounted for a general election with the National Government intact. The Labour members of the government, who were now virtually without a party, were in no position to resist. At first the Liberals did resist, for they feared that the government would be committed to a policy of tariffs; but eventually they were mollified by compromise proposals which left all parties free to make their separate appeals to the electorate.

A general election was held late in October. The result was a gigantic landslide in favour of the National Government, while the Conservatives had a huge majority over all other parties combined. The Labour Party was reduced to a pathetic rump of about fifty MPs, while MacDonald and the other erstwhile Labour leaders constituted a 'National Labour' Party with a dozen seats. The leader of that tiny group was to remain Prime Minister until 1935.

The Liberals were in a state of profound division. Not long before the National Government was formed, Simon and his principal associates had broken from the Liberal Party completely, and, just before the general election, they constituted themselves the 'Liberal Nationals'. The official Liberal Party, now headed by Sir Herbert Samuel, was at least clear that free trade must be defended; the Liberal Nationals or 'Simonites' had no such reservations. Lloyd George, whose health was by then more or less restored, reviled both groups, and sat among a minuscule opposition.

Immediately after the general election, there were significant changes in the government. A substantially higher proportion of offices passed to the Conservatives. The Liberal Nationals were brought into the government. Philip Snowden, who had been Chancellor of the Exchequer in both the 1929 Labour Government and the initial National Government, and whose commitment to free trade was not in doubt, took a viscountcy and went to the less influential post of Lord Privy Seal.

Soon the government commenced its assault on free trade. The story was a complex one, and will be studied largely through the cartoons. The upshot, however, was that in 1932 a general tariff of 10 per cent was imposed, with higher rates for certain items, while a few commodities remained on the 'free list'. Later in the same year, the free traders left the government, and in 1933 the Liberals went into formal opposition.

The immediate effects of all this were profound. Just as the Smoot-Hawley tariffs in the United States had encouraged a general move towards tariffs elsewhere, so also did the *Import Duties Act* of 1932 lead to a similar movement. In the longer term, the National Government profoundly influenced both the character of British politics and the course of world events. Secure with its massive majority, the National Government tended to ignore external criticism, while its critics were not subjected to the powerful discipline imposed upon people who realize that they may soon be required to vindicate their words in practice.

128

Cartoon 8.1 'Before you pick on me . . .'. *Evening Standard,*
London, 3 March 1930

At the beginning of 1930, Britain began to be affected by the Depression. In this cartoon, which appeared at the beginning of March, J.H. ('Jimmy') Thomas, the minister mainly responsible for the policy of the British government on unemployment, has evidently been reproved by John Bull, but seeks to excuse himself by explaining that his counterparts in other countries were encountering similar difficulties. Thomas was widely criticized by members of all parties – including his own Labour Party – for failing to tackle unemployment with more vigour, and in fact was moved to another job within the government three months after this cartoon appeared.

The association of Thomas with a dress suit was a joke used repeatedly in Low's cartoons. Thomas was of working-class origin, and had risen to prominence within the trade union movement, but apparently had a somewhat incongruous liking for that kind of attire.

The figure on the right would probably not be drawn in such a form by a modern British cartoonist, and certainly not by one with the advanced opinions and penetrating sensitivity of Low; but in that period it was common to represent Africans more or less as savages.

Cartoon 8.2 An extra one. *Evening Standard*, London, 22 May 1930

AN EXTRA ONE.

By May 1930, unemployment figures were a good deal worse than they had been a couple of months earlier. J. H. Thomas surveys the growing number in the dole queue, and suddenly notices a well-dressed man at the end – Sir Oswald Mosley.

Mosley's career had already been remarkable, and was later to develop in an even more astonishing manner. He was first elected for Harrow at the 'Coupon Election' of 1918, as a typical young ex-service Unionist with an aristocratic background. Then he became an Independent, and successfully defended his seat in that capacity in 1922 and 1923. He later moved to the Labour Party, and was returned for Smethwick at a by-election in 1926.

In the 1929 Labour Government, Mosley became a junior minister. He took a great interest in the unemployment question, making some radical representations to government colleagues on the matter. These were eventually rejected, and on 21 May Mosley resigned from the government, amid great publicity. This cartoon appeared on the following day. Not long afterwards, Mosley resigned from the Labour Party too. He established a 'New Party', which fared disastrously at the 1931 general election. Later he became leader of the British Union of Fascists.

Cartoon 8.3 It's safest to stand still. *Evening Standard*, London, 26 May 1930

RAMSAY: "WHAT SAY? YOU WANT TO GO SOMEWHERE? WELL, AREN'T YOU THE RECKLESS FELLOWS! DON'T YOU KNOW IT'S SAFETY WEEK?"

ITS SAFEST TO STAND STILL.

This cartoon is also by Low, and comments on the general stagnation of policy, particularly towards unemployment, which characterized the early period of the Depression.

Ramsay MacDonald, driver of the Labour taxi, looks up complacently from his newspaper, and fatuously defends the government's inactivity, while the passengers, 'Unemployment, Industry and Agriculture', show irritation at the Prime Minister's failure to help their plight. In the Conservative taxi, Stanley Baldwin also waits idly at the taxi rank, while passenger Lord Beaverbrook shows similar irritation. Beaverbrook was at that time meditating the establishment of a party of his own. Lloyd George's tiny Liberal scooter is perhaps inadequate, and there are no passengers; but at least the driver seems willing to do his best.

The receiver of the telephone is off the hook. MacDonald, at any rate, seems unwilling to accept any further disturbing enquiries.

Cartoon 8.4 A bad month for Caesars. *Daily Express*, London, 12 March 1931

A BAD MONTH FOR CÆSARS.

This cartoon alludes to the assassination of Julius Caesar on the ides of March – 15 March – 44 BC, and to Shakespeare's treatment of the incident. Cartoonist Strube's 'little man' functions as the soothsayer, who attempted unsuccessfully to warn Caesar of the fateful ides.

In March 1931, the leaders of all three political parties were facing great difficulties from their recent followers. James Maxton, a famous Labour 'left-winger', and Sir Oswald Mosley prepare to assassinate their 'Caesar', Prime Minister Ramsay MacDonald. The Liberal Sir John Simon, who was reaching the conclusion that his party should cooperate with Conservatives rather that attempting to influence the Labour Government, prepares to assassinate 'Caesar' Lloyd George.

To the right of the picture, Conservative 'Caesar' Stanley Baldwin – with pipe – is threatened by several conspirators. Lord Beaverbrook, proprietor of the *Daily Express* and a number of other newspapers, an erstwhile Conservative who was currently attempting to set up a party of his own with a strong 'Empire' flavour, creeps up behind him. Winston Churchill, who had been Chancellor of the Exchequer in the previous Conservative Government, but who was deeply alienated by the 'bipartisan' policy which the Conservative and Labour leadership were coming to favour for India, stands musingly at Baldwin's side. Behind the pillars, top-hatted conspirators, who are apparently meant to represent the old-fashioned 'reactionary' type of Conservatives, are lurking with sinister intent.

Although not all of these 'conspiracies' are directly attributable to the impact of the Depression, there can be little doubt that most of them were more or less linked with the destabilizing effect which it was producing on all parties.

All of the 'conspiracies' failed. Within a year or two, Maxton and Mosley were in the political wilderness, from which they never returned. Simon had a considerable political career ahead of him in the National Government, but he was execrated by the Liberals and his efforts had little effect on Lloyd George. Beaverbrook's 'Empire Party' was a complete flop, and the main result of Churchill's truculence was that he was excluded from political office until the outbreak of war in 1939, with the effect that his early warnings about Nazi Germany went largely unheeded.

Cartoon 8.5 'The Glorious Twelfth'. *News of the World*, London, 9 August 1931

"THE GLORIOUS TWELFTH!"

MR. PHILIP SNOWDEN (to Sir George May): "We've no choice, May; we must keep these birds down."

A Committee of five members of the Cabinet is considering the recommendations of Sir George May's National Economy Committee. Concerted action by all three parties has been suggested.

In this period, the *News of the World* was a serious newspaper which devoted its main attention to the reporting of important events.

This cartoon appeared shortly after the report of the Economy Committee, which had been set up by the government earlier in the year. That report was currently under consideration by the government. 'The Glorious Twelfth', the title of the cartoon, was 12 August, the date on which grouse shooting traditionally began.

Chancellor of the Exchequer Philip Snowden assures the Economy Committee's Chairman, Sir George May, that expenditure must be kept down, and prepares to shoot from the 'government butt', while other marksmen prepare to do the same from the Conservative and Liberal butts. The social services, which were likely targets for attack, attempt to hide.

The comment at the bottom of the cartoon is significant. In the ensuing fortnight, pressure for 'concerted action by all three parties' – effectively, the establishment of some kind of all-party coalition – became stronger and stronger.

Cartoon 8.6 The Government United take the field. *Daily Express*, London, 29 August 1931

THE GOVERNMENT UNITED TAKE THE FIELD.

On 24 August 1931, the Labour Government fell, and a National Government was formed – in the first instance as a genuine all-party government. This cartoon appeared a few days later. Ramsay MacDonald leads the team, and is followed by Stanley Baldwin, Sir Herbert Samuel, Neville Chamberlain, Philip Snowden and J. H. Thomas.

The team is being barracked by Labour Party critics, among whom may be recognized Arthur Henderson (with rattle, at the corner), Herbert Morrison (immediately behind Henderson's hat), George Lansbury (shouting 'Sez you!') and James Maxton (shouting at Chamberlain).

Strube commonly drew a 'little man' with spectacles and a moustache, with whom the reader was invited to identify. This time, the 'little man' enthusiastically cheers the new team.

Cartoon 8.7 The cat comes back! *News of the World,* London, 4 October 1931

THE CAT COMES BACK!

THE COOK (Mr. Baldwin) to THE-MAN-OF-ALL-WORK (Mr. Ramsay MacDonald): " You can't do better, Mac, than give this little fellow a chance!"

The Premier, it is understood, wants to appeal to the country at the head of a National Government on a policy which he calls " The Doctor's Mandate." This would include tariffs and any other expedient which might seem necessary to restore our financial and economic position.

MacDonald and his Labour associates, who had been denounced by their own party, were in no position to resist Conservative pressure for an early general election. This cartoon was drawn at a time when the decision for an election had not yet been taken, but it was fairly obvious that it soon would be.

Baldwin, the cook, urges a dubious MacDonald to accept the cat, 'Tariffs', to deal with mice – 'foreign traders' – who are demolishing the 'British trade balance cheese'. The housemaid – Sir Herbert Samuel, who was acting as Liberal leader during Lloyd George's illness – responds to Baldwin's suggestion with visible distaste.

In the event, the general election was held, as Baldwin had wished; but concession was made to Samuel's free trade predilections, in that the parties were authorized to fight it on their individual programmes, and there was no formal government commitment to tariffs.

Cartoon 8.8 The open goal. *News of the World*, London, 8 November 1931

THE OPEN GOAL.

JOHN BULL (yelling to the Prime Minister): " Shoot, Mac, shoot!"

Emergency measures are being urged upon the Government to deal with the unprecedented dumping which is now taking place in anticipation of tariffs.

This cartoon was drawn shortly after the 1931 general election. Most of the government's opponents had been defeated; two of the few survivors were Lloyd George and Labour's new leader, George Lansbury (foreground, right), both of whom are shown in a condition of considerable discomfort.

MacDonald is being urged by John Bull to shoot 'emergency measures' into the 'anti-dumping' goal – in other words, to take immediate action against to so-called 'dumping' of foreign goods.

Cartoon 8.9 Pay up – or stay out! *News of the World*, London, 22 November 1931

PAY UP—OR STAY OUT!

Mr. WALTER RUNCIMAN (President of the Board of Trade): "It's about time you paid your 'footing,' gentlemen. You have been on the Free list too long!"

The first Order under the Abnormal Importations Act, imposing 50 per cent duties on dumped articles of manufacture, comes into operation on Wednesday

The role of Walter Runciman in the debate over protection was remarkable. He had a considerable reputation as a free trader, but was one of those Liberals who had been far from happy with Lloyd George's leadership during the Labour Government. When the 'Liberal National' group was formed just before the election, Runciman joined it. Most Liberal Nationals had by this time become protectionists, but Runciman remained, at heart at least, a staunch free trader.

Immediately after the general election, the National Government was reconstituted, and the Liberal Nationals were brought in. Runciman became President of the Board of Trade, and his first task was to draw up an 'Abnormal Importations Bill', to deal with imports which were being rushed into the country in anticipation of tariffs. He probably disliked the task, but could console himself with the reflection that his Bill was only designed to remain in force for six months.

This cartoon really puts Runciman, the customs official, in a false position, for he certainly took no pleasure in what he was doing, but he probably reflected that it was better that he should be in charge of the measure than that it should be handled by an avowed protectionist.

Cartoon 8.10 Heroic deeds from history – No. 1. *Evening Standard*, London, 28 January 1932

After the *Abnormal Importations Act* was passed, the National Government set to work to devise a more permanent system of tariffs. Free traders in the government – the 'official' Liberals, headed by Samuel, and also Snowden from the National Labour Party – deeply opposed the idea, and were poised to resign. Then an 'agreement to differ' was devised, by which they remained free to speak and vote against the government's tariff proposals, and yet remained within the government.

Cartoon 8.10 (see page 140) is a cynical comment on the 'agreement to differ', explained by the inset at the top left. Leonidas and his Spartan hoplites at Thermopylae (480 BC) are, respectively, Sir Herbert Samuel, Sir Archibald Sinclair, Sir Donald Maclean and Philip – who had recently become Viscount – Snowden. They knew that the 'tariff hosts' were certain to proceed along the pass – but, technically, they had not abandoned it to the enemy.

The free trade ministers won little credit, and no long-term benefit, from accepting the 'agreement to differ'. Their free trade followers began to doubt their leadership, and before the year was out they had all left the National Government.

How far the British people swung from a positively free trade stance in the 1920s to a positive support for tariffs in the early 1930s is a matter of speculation. Throughout the whole period, there were substantial numbers of convinced free traders and convinced protectionists; but the issue was decided by people not firmly committed to either side. In the 1920s, they had tended to support free trade as the familiar 'status quo'; but, under impact of the Depression the people of Britain, like the people of Germany, cast around for a change. The Germans finished up with Hitler; the British finished up with protection. When most members of the National Government came out in favour of protection, most of the general public was prepared to go with them, without any deep conviction either way.

Neville Chamberlain, who was Chancellor of the Exchequer from November 1931 until he became Prime Minister in May 1937, played a critical part in the abandonment of free trade. Son of the redoubtable Joseph

HEROIC DEEDS FROM HISTORY — No 1.

(Copyright in all countries)

140

Cartoon 8.11 Thirty years on. *Punch*, London,
10 February 1932

THIRTY YEARS ON.

THE FISCAL BOY TO THE WAR HAS GONE.
IN THE FORWARD RANKS YOU'LL FIND HIM.
HIS FATHER'S SWORD HE HAS GIRDED ON
AND FLUNG FREE TRADE BEHIND HIM.

Chamberlain and half-brother of the former Foreign Secretary Sir Austen Chamberlain, Neville Chamberlain had a strong family interest in the tariff question.

This cartoon refers obliquely to Joseph Chamberlain's 'fiscal policy' – his 'tariff reform' campaign of 1903–6, where the first serious (though unsuccessful) attempt was made to shift Britain from free trade to protection. The readership of *Punch* in those days was largely drawn from the middle class and above, among whom there was probably a strong preponderance of people with Conservative and protectionist sympathies. Many were old enough to remember vividly the older battles. The lines parody an old Irish song, 'The Minstrel Boy'.

Cartoon 8.12 Little Bo-Peep has lost her sheep. *Evening Standard*, London, 16 February 1932

'Little Bo-Peep' – the 'free trade government supporter' – sought to defend all her sheep, but instead nearly all have been driven off by the protectionist Chancellor of the Exchequer, Neville Chamberlain, who is mounted on 'Import Duties Bill', and drives them with whip and dogs towards the compound '10 per cent general duty'. Under the new legislation, which was on its way through Parliament, most imports would pay a 10% duty, while some would pay heavier duties still – hence the buildings 'Extra Duty Dept.' and 'Special Extra Duty Dept.'.

Sir John Gilmour, Minister of Agriculture and Fisheries, proffers to Bo-Peep the tiny 'free list' of goods which will not be subject to import duties.

SPECIAL EXTRA DUTY DEPT.

EXTRA DUTY DEPT.

10% GENERAL DUTY

FREE LIST!

GILMOUR

FREETRADE GOVT. SUPPORTER

IMPORT DUTIES BILL

LITTLE BO-PEEP HAS LOST HER SHEEP.

(Copyright in all countries.)

143

9

The Nazi rise to power, 1923–33

In the light of what happened later, the early history of Nazism in Germany may be perceived as one of the most important series of events of the 1920s. At the very beginning, Nazism was an obscure movement of little general interest. By 1923, however, it was already attracting considerable attention from cartoonists and others, both in Germany and elsewhere. At the time, the two leading Nazi figures were seen to be Adolf Hitler and General Erich von Ludendorff. Ludendorff had been one of the most important German commanders in the First World War, ranking second only to Hindenburg. It was astonishing that a man with such a reputation was already regarded as no more than equal with the Austrian ex-corporal.

The nature of Nazism was by no means clearly defined or understood at that time: indeed, it attracted people with very disparate ideas. Many saw it as a 'monarchist' movement, which sought a Hohenzollern restoration and German revenge for the 1919 peace settlement. Some commentators, particularly in the Soviet Union, noticed a similarity with Mussolini's movement in Italy, and applied the label 'Fascist'; but it must not be thought that there was much sympathy between the two movements at the time.

There were several quite serious disturbances in Germany in the five years which followed the First World War. The year 1923, however, was critical in several ways. It witnessed the beginning of French occupation in the Ruhr and the highest level of post-war inflation. At such a time, it was not surprising that some kind of attempt should be made by extremist groups to seize power by force.

In November 1923, the Nazis staged what has become known as the Munich 'Beer-House *Putsch*'. The *putsch*, which involved considerable loss of life, was apparently designed as prelude to a 'march on Berlin'; but it proved a fiasco. The leaders were arrested and brought to trial. Ludendorff was acquitted, but Hitler was sentenced to a term of imprisonment. This period the future Führer spent in considerable luxury, and he devoted much of his time to writing *Mein Kampf*, which was later seen as the 'Bible' of Nazism.

In the later 1920s, Nazism was widely seen as a spent force. When Ludendorff stood for presidency of the Republic after Ebert's death, he only secured about 1 per cent of the votes cast. In the Reichstag elections of 1928, the Nazis only won a dozen seats, worse even than their poor showing of December 1924. They seemed to be far overshadowed not only by a miscellany of parties of the 'left' and 'centre', but also even on the 'right' – by the German National Party.

It was the Great Depression which began in October 1929 which gave real impetus to the Nazis. Even before the slump commenced, there were signs of rising unemployment in Germany; but when the slump arrived there was an enormous increase. Although a measure of social security had existed in Germany ever since Bismarck's time, it was far from adequate, and there was a widespread feeling of bitter disillusionment with the various coalitions of more or less democratic parties which ruled Germany.

The political beneficiaries were the Nazis and – to a smaller degree – the Communists. In the Reichstag elections of September 1930, the Nazis and the Communists won 107 and 77 seats respectively, becoming the second and third parties of the state. Neither of them felt much distress at the simultaneous rise of the party which they proclaimed to be their ultimate enemy. The Nazis realized that Communist advances would dispose many people to move in their own direction, while the Communists were convinced that an eventual Nazi Government would create conditions which would produce the revolution they desired.

Even before the 1930 elections, political conditions had become so difficult, with intense economic problems and a multiplicity of parties in the Reichstag, that the Chancellor, Heinrich Brüning, commenced the dangerous expedient of 'government by decree' instead of passing through the ordinary procedure of legislation. After the election, no other form of government was possible. Brüning was a member of the Catholic 'centre', and the economic ideas to which he gave effect were deflationary; but members of other non-totalitarian parties were not disposed to defy him too much, lest even worse should befall. By general agreement, the democratic parties abandoned the normal machinery of parliamentary democracy as unworkable. Meanwhile, the economic situation, and in particular unemployment, grew steadily worse. This relieved Germany of at least one burden; for it was universally agreed that further reparations were out of the question for a long time to come, and probably for ever.

In April 1932, Paul von Hindenburg reached the end of his seven-year term of office, and new presidential elections were required. The old man – he was already 84 – was persuaded to stand again. In 1925, he had been seen as the candidate of the 'right' (see Cartoon 6.5); in 1932 he was recognized as the only man who could possibly stop Hitler, and received general support from the democratic parties. Hindenburg was elected by a substantial majority, with Hitler running second and the Communist a poor third.

By this time, street battles between rival gangs of toughs, nominally linked to political parties, had become intense. Shortly after Hindenburg's re-election, Chancellor Brüning attempted to ban the Nazi 'paramilitary' organizations, the SA and the SS. The President failed to give him the necessary support, and Brüning resigned. The new Chancellor, Franz von Papen, was not a politician at all, but was very much the personal nominee of Hindenburg.

The Nazis offered support to Papen on condition that their organized thugs should be legalized again, and that fresh elections should be held. Those new elections, of July 1932, gave the Nazis 230 seats, more than twice as many as they had held before, and more than the next two parties, the Social Democrats and the Communists, combined. The Nazis and the Communists, both avowed enemies of parliamentary democracy, now constituted between them an overall majority of the Reichstag.

Further elections were held in November 1932. The Nazis slipped back substantially, but remained the largest single party by a large margin. On the 'left', the Social Democrats lost ground and the Communists advanced, so that the gap between those two parties was small. Papen's position soon became impossible, and he resigned office.

The new Chancellor, General Kurt von Schleicher, was a very 'political' soldier, who at one time had contemplated an alliance between the army and the Nazis, but who by this time had fallen foul of Hitler. He then fell foul of the President as well, and soon resigned. There was only one possible successor, and on 30 January 1933 Hitler became Chancellor. He was still far from being dictator; his first Cabinet included only three avowed Nazis, and he could certainly not govern without a good deal of support from other politicians.

Cartoon 9.1 V tesnote i v obide. *Izvestiya*, Moscow,
26 September 1923

It was predictable that French action in the Ruhr would produce some
virulent movement of protest in Germany.

This is an early Soviet cartoon about the Nazis, which was drawn some
time before the Nazis made their first attempt to seize power. The question
is asked at the bottom, 'Who will provide the next ballast?' The balloon
'Germaniya' is losing height, and is coming dangerously close to a rough
sea. The pilot is about to jettison the ballast 'passive resistance' – i.e.
non-violent resistance to the occupying French forces in the Ruhr. The
other two passengers in the balloon, one a tough-looking worker and the

other an absurd-looking man wearing the Nazi swastika at his neck, square up to each other.

If the German government cannot gain enough height by abandoning 'passive resistance', then somebody must be dropped as ballast, or all will drown. The Nazi and the worker, who obviously hate each other, are each determined to push the other over. A Soviet cartoon would identify a 'worker' with a 'class-conscious worker' – that is, a Communist. The implication is that a struggle to the death between Nazis and Communists will soon develop. At the time when this cartoon was drawn there was no evidence that either of them had anything like enough support to give them a serious chance of taking control of Germany, but the cartoonist is attempting to prophesy what will happen in the future.

The Nazi's attire is curious. The swastika is familiar enough, but he wears a Prussian helmet of the wartime period, and this carries the monogram 'W', which implies that he is a monarchist, seeking the restoration of the exiled Kaiser Wilhelm II. The early Nazis did include some people who desired a restoration of the monarchy, but also other people whose ideology was not monarchist at all. The character of the Nazi Party was still by no means clearly defined; but it was certainly aggressively nationalist and deeply opposed to the Communists.

Cartoon 9.2 A la manière de Ludendorf[f]. *Le Canard Enchaîné*, Paris, 14 November 1923

A LA MANIERE DE LUDENDORF

— *Vite ! Nous sommes victorieux, le coup d'Etat a réussi... Nous n'avons plus qu'à [... le camp !*

This cartoon, 'In the manner of Ludendorff', appeared almost immediately after the attempted Nazi *putsch* of November 1923, when it was apparent that it had failed, but when the full consequences and implications were far from clear.

A Nazi comes to Ludendorff in desperation. He addresses him in soldierly slang, which may be rendered in somewhat more polite terms as 'Quick! We are victorious, the *coup d'état* has succeeded.... There is nothing we can do now but run away!'

During the *putsch*, Hitler made a speech in the course of which he said, 'The morrow will either see a German National Government ruling over Germany or it will see us dead.' Some of the Nazis were killed; but Hitler and Ludendorff both fled from the scene of the crime and were arrested later. Thus running away was action 'in the manner of Ludendorff'.

Cartoon 9.3 Die Gesundung kommt aus Bayern.
Simplicissimus, Munich, 3 December 1923

Die Gesundung kommt aus Bayern

Wenn die Brände von links und von rechts erloschen sind, wird sich aus der Asche leuchtend der Vogel Phönix erheben.

This cartoon also comments on the Munich *putsch* of November 1923. It was drawn, however, at a time when the situation was rather clearer than when the earlier French drawing was produced. The Bavarian von Kahr (left), Hitler (centre) and von Ludendorff (right) emerge unhappily from the wreckage of the fire. The beer-hall, site of the Nazi violence, is marked by scattered tankards and bottles. A phoenix emerges, though with a singed tail.

The title, 'Health comes from Bavaria', is in evident relief at the Nazis' failure. The words at the bottom confirm the message: 'When the fires of the left and the right are extinguished, then the phoenix bird will escape from the shining ashes.' The association of von Kahr with the escapade was unintentional, brief and confused. He was a Bavarian monarchist, whose interest was in restoration of the local Wittelsbach dynasty, rather than the Hohenzollern Empire or – still less – establishment of a Hitler dictatorship. He soon repudiated any kind of link with the Nazis, and was eventually murdered by them in 1934.

Simplicissimus had ridiculed the 'left-wing' Spartacists in an earlier cartoon (Cartoon 2.5); now it ridiculed the 'right-wing' Nazis.

Cartoon 9.4 Fashistskoe znamya . . . . *Izvestiya*, Moscow,
15 November 1923

ФАШИСТСКОЕ ЗНАМЯ В ИСПРАВЛЕННОМ И ДОПОЛНЕННОМ ВИДЕ.

This Soviet cartoon suggests a 'modification of the Fascist banner', and
reflects on the confusion which attended the unsuccessful Nazi *putsch* in
Bavaria. Hitler (bottom left) shoots at von Kahr, who fires at von Ludendorff. Ludendorff fires at General von Seeckt, who fires at Hitler.

Seeckt, who was playing a major part in creating the remodelled army
during this period, was certainly no friend of democracy; but he had
recently come under bitter attack from the Nazis, and there seems some
reason for thinking that he would have resisted a Nazi 'march on Berlin'
by force if necessary.

Soviet literature was disposed to use both the word 'Fascist' and the
Nazi swastika in a much wider context than did most other commentators,
and applied both the word and the symbol to many people whom Mussolini's Fascists and the German Nazis would have repudiated indignantly.

Cartoon 9.5 Die Drachensaat. *Vorwärts*, Berlin, 18 June 1924

Die Drachensaat.

Ludendorff-Kadmos: „Aufklärung im Weſten? Verflucht! Ich brauche Regenwetter für meine Saat!"

This cartoon appeared in the German Social Democratic newspaper Vorwärts. The Nazi von Ludendorff, in the character of the Greek hero Kadmos (Cadmus), sows the dragon's teeth from which armed men will spring. Behind him are swastika-bedecked steel helmets, preparing to rise from the ground.

Ludendorff bemoans, 'Clearing up in the west? Damn it! I need rainy weather for my sowing [of seed]!' In the western sky are signs of improving weather. In France, Poincaré's government had recently departed, and his successors were a good deal more amenable to reaching an amicable arrangement over the linked questions of the Ruhr and reparations. The Dawes Plan had been promulgated in the United States, and had recently been accepted in principle by the French and German governments. Ludendorff required 'rainy weather' – bad economic conditions, foreign aggression – to encourage the Nazi movement, which was sure to abate if conditions continued to improve.

The reference to a Greek legend in a newspaper aimed largely at working-class readers is a striking reflection on the high general level of German education. It is difficult to imagine a British, French or American newspaper aimed at a similar readership being equally confident that the allusion would have been understood.

It is possible that a further subtlety was intended. The name Kadmos has been read to mean 'from the east'. Ludendorff came from Posen – now Poznan – which was in eastern Germany at the time, but had become part of the 'Polish Corridor' under the Versailles arrangements. A contrast is perhaps drawn between the wishes of the 'easterner' to recover his homeland, and the improved weather in the west which makes war, which would be essential for such a development, less likely.

This is another German cartoon from the spring of 1924, expressing the idea that the Nazis were a spent force. The title is 'First of April' and it is intended as an 'April Fool' jest.

In his 'entry to Berlin', Hitler is being crowned with a laurel wreath by a cherub, and is being announced by a herald, both portrayed in the baroque manner. He is flanked by a medieval Teutonic knight on one side, and a barbarian Germanic warrior on the other. The barbarian is assaulting a civilian, who is probably meant to be a Jew. Hitler leads Friedrich Ebert, the German President, in chains. In the background is the Brandenburg Gate, the most familiar Berlin landmark.

The figures accompanying Hitler are from different periods of German history, and allude obliquely to the Nazi disposition to romanticize all things German, most particularly those associated with violence and war.

Although the cartoon was designed to show the absurdity of Hitler's pretensions, it was to prove grimly prophetic. The one significant error was that President Ebert died early in the following year, and therefore was spared a part in Hitler's triumph.

Cartoon 9.6 Der erste April. *Simplicissimus*, Munich,
1 April 1924

Der erste April

(Th. Th. Heine)

Hitlers Einzug in Berlin

Cartoon 9.7 Strange bedfellows. *New York Times,* 14 December 1924

STRANGE BEDFELLOWS

An American comment on the German elections of December 1924. The Communists and 'Monarchists' (a term which seems here to mean 'Nazis' – a common misunderstanding of Nazi ideology at the time) have both suffered electoral injuries for which they have been put to bed. The two movements generally hated each other (although on certain occasions they collaborated), and in that sense they were 'strange bedfellows'.

The second German general election of 1924 showed a marked swing away from the extreme parties, and benefited the moderate political groups. The Nazis had but fourteen seats and the Communists forty-five in a Reichstag of 489.

Cartoon 9.8 Gebet der Vaterländischen. *Vorwärts*, Berlin,
20 May 1926

Gebet der Vaterländischen.

„Und gib uns einen kommunistischen Putsch, damit auch wir putschen können. Amen."

'Prayer of the fatherlanders' is a good illustration of how the Nazis looked
to the German 'moderate left' in the mid-1920s.

The Nazis are worshipping before an altar, on which the swastika is
set in place of the cross – with candles beside it and rifles in front. Nazi
attitudes to religion varied, but some were blatantly pagan rather than
irreligious in the ordinary sense. The judiciary in the background look
reverently towards the symbol, while the congregation kneels in prayer.

All the worshippers are male, but they are very mixed. Two are dressed
as Germanic warriors of the Dark Ages or earlier – an allusion to the
pagan romanticism of some Nazis. One wears the uniform and spurs of
a cavalry officer – reference to the appeal which Nazism made to some
old-fashioned militarists. Others are well-dressed, evidently wealthy, civilians, but some seem to derive from the lower middle classes, the group
which had suffered badly as a result of inflation. One member of the
congregation is much younger than the others, and seems to have sticking-
plaster on his face. He is probably meant to be one of those Nazi youths
who were often engaged in street battles with political opponents.

The prayer is 'And give us a Communist *putsch*, that we also may stage
a *putsch*.' All of the Nazis in the cartoon were hoping for Communist
violence, as in the five years immediately following the end of the war,
as an excuse for violence of their own.

When this cartoon was drawn, the Nazis seemed to have lapsed from
a real threat to something of a joke in Germany – not a serious challenge
to the democratic republic.

Cartoon 9.9 Der grosse Jammer. *Vorwärts*, Berlin, 25 May 1928

Der grosse Jammer.

Auch der „Erbfeind" weint dem Bürgerblock seine Tränen nach.

This cartoon in the Social-Democratic newspaper *Vorwärts* commemorates the German 1928 general election, which resulted in a considerable swing towards the 'moderate left' and away from the more conservative *Rechtsblock*.

At the grave of 'our deeply beloved *Rechtsblock*', there is a wreath from various German politicians of the 'right' – which might be expected – but there are also wreaths from 'French chauvinists', 'your hereditary enemy', and 'Polish nationalists'. The implication is that these external forces, hostile to Germany, were stimulated by policies of the *Rechtsblock*, but will in future lose influence in their own countries as the new Reichstag pursues more peaceful and less provocative policies.

The implication seems less than just. Whatever may be said of the domestic policy of the *Rechtsblock*, the Foreign Minister Gustav Stresemann won a great international reputation as a man of peace, and in fact remained in office when a new ministry further to the 'left' was formed after the election. His death in the following year is widely regarded as an unmitigated disaster.

Cartoon 9.10 Brünings kleine Scherzartikel. *Vorwärts*, Berlin, 16 September 1930

Brünings kleine Scherzartikel.

Damit können Sie sich stundenlang amüsieren!

Three German cartoons (Cartoons 9.10, 9.11 and 9.12) about the German general election of September 1930 and its result.

The first cartoon, 'Brüning's little toys' is from *Vorwärts*. It shows the Nazi propagandist Goebbels and the Communist Thälmann as jack-in-the-box toys, assailing each other with the Nazi salute and the Communist clenched-fist salute respectively. The wording at the bottom reads, roughly, 'With it you can amuse yourself for hours!' The two parties were bitterly critical of each other – hence the rudely stuck-out tongues of the politicians. The cartoonist is evidently attempting to show that both of those parties were rather absurd, and not worthy of serious consideration by the electorate.

Cartoon 9.11 Hallo! Wie lange . . . . *Völkisher Beobachter*,
Munich, 16 October 1930

The second cartoon is from the Nazi newspaper, *Völkischer Beobachter*,
and was drawn at a time when politicians were considering the form of
government which should be set up after the election. The Nazi, with '6.5
million Nazi votes' behind him, assails Chancellor Heinrich Brüning, and
demands how long he proposes to muddle on. The message at the bottom
declares that the Catholic *Zentrum* – Brüning's own party – is prepared
to sell its soul to the 'dissident' Braun. Otto Braun, Social Democratic
Prime Minister of Prussia, in the bottom right of the picture, is apparently
cast in the role of Mephistopheles, persuading Brüning, as Faust, to sign
the compact selling his soul.

Cartoon 9.12 Le nouveau Reichstag. *Nebelspalter*, Rorschach, copied in *L'Europe Nouvelle*, 1 November 1930

Le nouveau Reichstag

107 nationaux-socialistes + 41 nationalistes + 77 communistes = 225 députés antiparlement-aires.

(Extrait de *Nebelspalier*, de Rorschach.)

The third cartoon, 'The new Reichstag', meditates on the results of the election. '107 National Socialists [Nazis] + 41 Nationalists + 77 Communists = 225 anti-parliamentary deputies'. As has been noted, both Nazis and Communists made considerable advances at the election. The Nationalists of Alfred Hugenberg were a more 'reactionary' party, harking back rather to the pre-1914 days. Today they may be regarded as a great deal less sinister and dangerous than the others; but, prior to 1930, they had been a much larger body than the Nazis.

Cartoon 9.13 Goebbels und die Reichspräsidentenwahl. *Simplicissimus*, Munich, 6 March 1932

Goebbels und die Reichspräsidentenwahl

„O nein, o nein, o nein, o nein!
Mein Kandidat muß größer sein!"

At the German presidential elections of April 1932, von Hindenburg stood for re-election. His most serious challenger was Hitler.

In this German cartoon, 'Goebbels and the Reich-presidential election', which was drawn at an early stage of the election, Goebbels, chief Nazi propagandist, is confronted with the enormous figure of Hindenburg. In the hope of producing a candidate of comparable stature, he is attempting to blow air into the rival figure. He chants, 'O no, o no, o no, o no! My candidate must become bigger!'

Hindenburg was elected with a majority of something like six million over Hitler, with the Communist Thälmann far behind.

Cartoon 9.14 SS.- und SA.-Verbot. *Simplicissimus*, Munich, 1 May 1932

S S.- und S A.-Verbot

[Th. Th. Heine]

„Huhuhu — die bösen Onkels haben uns unsere Soldaten weggenommen, nun können wir nicht mehr Bürgerkrieg spielen!"

Two cartoons (Cartoons 9.14 and 9.15) about Chancellor Brüning's efforts to ban the Nazi paramilitary organizations, the SA and the SS.

The first, 'Banning of SA and SS', appeared at the beginning of May 1932. Hitler and two other Nazis – probably Goebbels and Goering – weep loudly as their toy soldiers are taken away from them. 'Boohoo! The wicked uncles have taken away our soldiers – and now we can't play at civil war any more!' The Nazi street gangs had been terrorizing political opponents, and organizing street battles against them, for a long time. Brüning's decision to ban them was an act of great political courage, and represented perhaps the last chance of saving the republic from Nazi control.

Tragically, Brüning did not receive the support from Hindenburg which was essential if the ban was to take effect, and he resigned office. In the second cartoon, 'Brüning's farewell', the Chancellor is disappearing through a trap-door in the floor. As he goes, he addresses the President with a grim smile, 'Goodbye, Mr Reichspresident, and send me a picture postcard from the Third Reich some time!'

Nazis were coming to describe the state which they proposed to rule as the 'Third Reich'. The First Reich was the Holy Roman Empire, which had lasted from 800 to 1806, and for most of the time German-speaking people formed a major part of the Empire. The Second Reich was the German Empire set up by Bismarck, which lasted from 1871 to 1918. Nazis declared that the Third Reich, like the First, would last for a thousand years.

This cartoon suggests that Brüning recognized that his own departure would usher in the Third Reich at no distant date. If so, he was correct. Within eight months, Hitler was Chancellor in Brüning's place.

Cartoon 9.15 Brünings Abschied. *Simplicissimus*, Munich, 19 June 1932

Cartoon 9.16 Mutter Germania ertrinkt. *Simplicissimus*, Munich, 9 October 1932

Mutter Germania ertrinkt —

(E. Schilling)

während ihre Söhne sich darum streiten, wer ihr den Rettungsring zuwerfen soll.

'Mother Germania is drowning!' is the title of this German cartoon of October 1932, which was drawn in the period between the two general elections of that year. The Social Democrat (holding a cudgel), Chancellor von Papen (top right), ex-Chancellor Brüning (in front of him), and a Nazi and a Communist, each armed with a knife, are all fighting (as the legend at the bottom points out) about who shall throw the lifebelt to drowning Germania.

The cartoonist seems far from convinced as to which – if any – of them should throw the lifebelt, but feels pity for his country's plight in the appalling economic conditions of the time.

In one sense, this attitude seems encouraging, for the cartoonist is clearly not a convinced Nazi. Yet, from another point of view, the drawing is much less encouraging. Like many cartoons of the period between 1919 and Hitler's assumption of power in 1933, it contrasts 'Germany', which deserves the reader's sympathy, and the contending politicians and political groupings, which are seen as merely divisive. People adopting that attitude could very easily move on to the view that any contender who secured overall control deserved their wholehearted support, for he would then represent 'Germany'. There is much reason for thinking that many Germans who had not supported Hitler in his earlier struggle later swung towards him for reasons of 'patriotism'.

Cartoon 9.17 Germanias Weihnachtsbescherung.
Simplicissimus, Munich, 25 December 1932

Germanias Weihnachtsbescherung *(Th. Th. Heine)*

„Und hier, mein liebes Kind, das schönste Weihnachtsgeschenk: ein lebendiger General! Hoffentlich gefällt er dir. Ein Umtausch kommt zunächst nicht in Betracht."

When von Papen resigned as Chancellor in November 1932 – much to Hindenburg's dismay – General Kurt von Schleicher was appointed in his place. The caption – 'Germany's Christmas present' – is friendly. So are the fatherly words with which the old President addresses Germania: 'And here, my dear child, is the best Christmas present: a real live General! I hope it will please you. For the time being, an exchange cannot be contemplated.'

Von Schleicher pleased few people. Anti-Nazis were deeply suspicious of the sympathy which he had shown for an understanding with the Nazis not long before, and deplored his military connections. The Nazis were disposed to see him as an enemy or even an apostate. When Schleicher attempted to introduce rural land reform, the landowning Junkers, and

168

Cartoon 9.18 The temporary triangle. *Punch*, London,
8 February 1933

THE TEMPORARY TRIANGLE.

Von HINDENBURG AND VON PAPEN (*together*)—
"FOR HE'S A JOLLY GOOD FELLOW,
FOR HE'S A JOLLY GOOD FELLOW,
FOR HE'S A JOLLY GOOD FE-EL-LOW,
(*Aside*: "Confound him!")
AND SO SAY BOTH OF US!"

not least the President's son Otto, condemned it as 'rural Bolshevism'.

Thus the new Chancellor's position was precarious. When he resigned, towards the end of January 1933, there was no available alternative to Hitler.

In 1934, von Schleicher, like another of Hitler's brief associates, von Kahn, was murdered by the Nazis.

On 30 January 1933, von Hindenburg appointed Hitler as Chancellor. The first Hitler Cabinet was by no means overwhelmingly Nazi.

As the British cartoon on the previous page (Cartoon 9.18) suggests, Hitler could only maintain his position by receiving some kind of support from Hindenburg, and from the ex-Chancellor von Papen, who took office in the new government. Neither of them liked the appointment, but there was really no other available candidate likely to command popular enthusiasm, and both hoped to exert some kind of control over him.

10

Japan, 1921–33

Japan had fought on the Allied side in the First World War, and received some former German colonies thereafter. Even at the time of the peace conferences, however, there was some feeling among Japanese people that their country was not receiving the recognition it deserved from the Allies (see Cartoon 1.8). At the Washington Conference of 1921–2, however, there was general agreement between the powers who had interests in the Pacific area, and the main disputes seemed to have been resolved.

Soon new problems arose. In 1924, the United States passed legislation excluding Asians from emigrating to the United States. Japan deeply resented this policy, not so much as injurious to her interests – more Japanese had returned to their own country from America than had emigrated over the previous twenty years – but as a national affront.

China had been more or less disintegrating for a long time, and many Japanese were disposed to look in that direction for possible economic or territorial expansion. The Great Depression, however, greatly accentuated Japanese interest in China. The Japanese silk industry was particularly hit by trade restrictions imposed by the United States and China, and many people suffered great privations.

Manchuria was ostensibly a Chinese province, although in practice the Chinese control was weak. Across Manchuria there ran a railway over which Japan had rights recognized by international treaties. In September 1931, an obscure quarrel arose between local Japanese and Chinese units in connection with the railway. This soon escalated to a full-scale conflict, whose real issue was the control of Manchuria. In a fairly short time, Manchuria was converted into a nominally independent state, renamed Manchukuo, under strong Japanese influence.

The matter clearly called for League of Nations consideration. In February 1933 the Lytton Report appeared, and was adopted by the League shortly afterwards. The most important conclusions of the report were hostile to Japan's view of the matter. There was, however, no way in which this opinion could be made effective, for nobody was able or willing to coerce Japan by military force. Japan retorted by declaring her intention to leave the League of Nations. The whole affair was, of course, disastrous to the League's moral authority.

Cartoon 10.1 The Pacific bubble. *Bystander*, London, 16 November 1921

THE PACIFIC BUBBLE   BY ALFRED LEETE

At the Washington Conference of 1921–2, the major powers in the Pacific region reached what looked like a broadly based agreement about their interests in the area.

In this cartoon of late 1921, representatives of the United States, Britain, Japan and France are gathered in a ring, and inflate together the soap-bubble 'disarmament'. Evidently the cartoonist was not convinced that their efforts would have any degree of permanence. Nevertheless, they seemed to be cooperating in a common plan.

Cartoon 10.2 Le citoyen américain. *Yorodsu*, Tokyo, copied by *L'Europe Nouvelle*, Paris, 26 July 1924

Le citoyen américain : « Voilà des nuages menaçants ! »
[La voile de la barque porte l'inscription : *Exclusion des Japonais.*
Celles des nuages signifient : *Aliénation de la sympathie du monde, et Union des peuples asiatiques.*]

(Extrait du *Yorodzu*, de Tokio.)

This Japanese cartoon comments on the American decision to curtail Japanese immigration to the United States.

The American vessel carries on its sail the words 'Exclusion of the Japanese'. The navigator points with alarm at the menacing clouds which carry the words 'Alienation of world sympathy' and 'Union of the Asian peoples'.

The message of the cartoon is that this American policy would be taken as an insult by the Japanese, and also by other Asians who were similarly excluded. It is an early sign of the developing alienation between the two countries, who had fought on the same side in the war which ended only six years earlier.

Years later, during the Second World War, the Japanese developed the idea of a 'co-prosperity scheme' involving other countries in the Pacific area, under Japanese leadership. This cartoon foreshadows that idea.

173

Cartoon 10.3 L'Amérique, le Japon et la vieille Europe.
Mucha, Warsaw, copied by *L'Europe Nouvelle*, Paris,
30 August 1924

L'oncle Sam au Japon : « Voyez donc cette vieille Europe :
elle est tout près de rendre l'âme ! C'est alors qu'il y aura
beaucoup de place pour vous sur la terre ! »

(Extrait du *Mucha*, de Varsovie.)

This Polish cartoon takes a rather different view of the American exclusion of Japanese from entry to the United States. Uncle Sam says to Japan, 'Look at that old Europe: she is quite ready to give up the ghost! Then there will be plenty of place for you on the earth!'

The direct message is obvious; but perhaps there is an indirect suggestion as well. If 'old Europe' is indeed 'ready to give up the ghost', then presumably the extensive and rich European possessions in the Far East will become available for Japanese settlement.

American policy was gradually becoming hostile to Japan; but the Americans had no sympathy with the European imperialists, and were quite willing to see their influence collapse.

Cartoon 10.4 Dans le Pacifique. *Nichi-nichi Shimbun*, Tokyo, copied by *L'Europe Nouvelle*, Paris, 22 March 1930

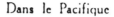

L'Amérique, les yeux tournés vers le Japon: 'J'ai fait une faute en ne dévorant pas ce ver il y a des années; maintenant, il est trop gros.'
(Extrait du *Nichi-nichi Shumbun*, de Tokio.)

This Japanese cartoon is striking because it was drawn long before the Manchurian crisis of 1931–3. The bird America, looking towards Japan, says 'I made a mistake in not eating that worm some years ago; now it's too big!' Perhaps the bird is meant to be an American eagle; if so, its bill is much too large, and eagles are not likely to eat worms if larger prey is available.

America is coming to perceive Japan as a serious rival to her interests in the Pacific, of whom she cannot dispose easily.

Cartoon 10.5 Humour chinois. *Hsiao jen hao*, Shanghai, copied by *L'Europe Nouvelle*, Paris, 10 October 1931

Humour chinois.

Les médecins japonais, qui prétendent soigner la
Chine, la découpent en petits morceaux.
(Extrait de *Hsiao jen hao*, de Changhaï.)

This Chinese cartoon was drawn shortly after fighting began in Manchuria in 1931. The Japanese doctors, who are pretending to help China, are cutting her into small pieces.

It took the League of Nations a very long time to study the Manchurian question, but, when at last the 'Lytton Report' on the subject was debated, the League decided that Japan was, on balance, in the wrong.

Japan, the truculent pupil in Cartoon 10.6, retorted by declaring her intention to leave the League of Nations.

Cartoon 10.6 The ultimatum. *Punch*, London,
7 December 1932

THE ULTIMATUM.

JAPAN. "IF YOU GO ON SAYING I'M NAUGHTY, I SHALL LEAVE THE CLASS."

Cartoon 10.7 The stars of the Geneva constellation. *Punch*, London, 8 February 1933

MANCHUKUO

[The stars of the Geneva Constellation, in view of the fact that the sun *will* keep on rising, doubt whether they ought to offer any definitely partisan opposition to prevent it from doing so.]

Sir JOHN SIMON (Great Britain), M. PAUL BONCOUR (France), Baron ALOISI (Italy), M. MOTTA (Switzerland), M. BENES (Czecho-Slovakia), M. PAUL HYMANS (Belgium) and Mr. MATSUOKA (Japan).

Cartoon 10.8 Japan und der Völkerbund. *Simplicissimus,* Munich, 22 January 1933

Japan und der Völkerbund

„Pfui doch, Japsi, du sollst es der Tante doch wenigstens immer vorher sagen, wenn du wieder mal ein bißchen Krieg spielen willst!"

These cartoons (Cartoons 10.7, 10.8 and 10.9) present three views of the failure of the League of Nations to take effective action against Japan in the aftermath of the Manchurian conflict.

The *Punch* cartoon is bland. The 'stars of the Geneva constellation' are the Foreign Ministers of various powers gathered at the League of Nations headquarters in Geneva. At the bottom, Japanese Foreign Minister Matsuoka is at the centre of the Japanese 'rising sun'. All have agreed that nothing can be done about the situation.

179

Cartoon 10.9 The Cat and Mouse Act (new version). *Evening Standard*, London, 17 February 1933

THE CAT AND MOUSE ACT (NEW VERSION). *(Copyright in all countries.)*

In the German cartoon, 'Japan and the League of Nations', the various children are in charge of a senile League of Nations. Japan is making a murderous attack on China. The League reprimands him in a fatuous manner: 'Tut, tut, Japsy, you should warn Auntie the next time you want to start a little war.' The plant in the window grows from a barrel of 'caution powder'. The other children, including one wearing a Soviet red star in his cap and another who seems to be an Italian 'blackshirt' – i.e. Fascist – are drawing their own conclusions.

The *Evening Standard* (Low) cartoon is even more astringent. The Japanese mouse roars, and terrifies the cat 'World statesmanship'. The truth is that most 'world statesmen' were at that moment preoccupied with other matters. Less than three weeks earlier, Hitler had become Chancellor of Germany. The original 'Cat and Mouse Act', to which the cartoon alludes, was a piece of British legislation of 1913 designed to deal with 'suffragettes' convicted of violent crimes who went on hunger-strike in prison.

11

A time of conferences, 1925–33

The question of disarmament constantly recurred during the inter-war period. In theory, the disarmament of ex-enemy countries prescribed by the peace treaties was to be a prelude to general disarmament by the Allies, which would take place just as soon as it could safely be done.

The Germans, however, complained that there was no sign of the Allies disarming. France was the most heavily-armed country on the European continent, and even countries like Czechoslovakia and Poland, which had been set up after the war with Allied support, had considerable armaments. The importance of arms to French policy was brought out very sharply in 1923. France was able to invade the Ruhr, despite the fact that not only Germany, but Britain too, felt considerable concern at her actions. In the 1920s, the Germans seemed genuinely fearful of military action not only by France but by the newer countries as well.

Pressure for disarmament came from many places. A great many people in all lands, particularly young people, were attracted to a pacifist or semi-pacifist ideology. They were disposed to regard great armaments not merely as a means of waging war, but as a positive cause of war. Even people who were not impressed by such arguments doubted the wisdom, and deplored the expense, of massive armaments, and were anxious to see them drastically reduced by international agreement.

At the Locarno Conference of 1925, it was agreed that preparations should be made for a World Disarmament Conference, which would be held at a date in the rather remote future. As time went on, the idea of such a conference acquired increasing force. Not only the League of Nations countries, but the United States and the Soviet Union as well, indicated that they were willing to participate.

At an early stage in the preliminary negotiations, the serious problem of 'equivalence' arose. Nations did not all have the same kind of armaments. How could one balance, for example, the military worth of a tank against that of a big gun, or of a battleship against a squadron of aeroplanes? It soon became apparent that there was no satisfactory way of assessing the equivalence of these weapons. Nevertheless, it did seem that much might be done without resolving such difficult questions.

The World Disarmament Conference eventually opened in February 1932. In one sense, that date seemed a propitious moment. Most countries

181

were in the depths of economic depression. Armaments cost a great deal of money, and there was much sense in attempting to save that money if possible.

Very soon, the conference began to run into trouble. The critical argument lay between France and Germany. The Germans took their stand on 'equality of rights'. Germany, they argued, had been forcibly disarmed in 1919. She attended the current conference as an equal with other countries, and would not countenance any arrangement which left her in an inferior position once the conference was over. The French countered this argument by a plea for security. France had been twice invaded by Germans within living memory. French security was paramount. No arrangement would be countenanced which diminished that security.

Towards the end of 1932, the conference nearly broke down over this dispute. With some difficulty, the British devised an acceptable form of words, and brought both countries back to the negotiating table.

By this time, enormous problems overhung the conference. In the course of 1932, the Nazis had established themselves as by far the strongest single party in Germany, although they had not yet taken office. German negotiators dared not make concessions which might tip the political scales in the Nazis' favour; conversely, the French were more jittery than ever about the threat to their security. Japan had already more or less succeeded in imposing her will on China, and was in the process of defying the League of Nations over the Manchurian settlement.

Hitler took office in Germany in January 1933, but this did not produce any immediate collapse of international cooperation. The Disarmament Conference continued to meet, while, in the summer of 1933, two other important international conferences were held.

At Lausanne, agreement was reached between the European countries on the matter of reparations. The form of this agreement was seen by the Americans as a shady conspiracy to thwart their legitimate claims, and by many Germans as a craven acknowledgement of the moral validity of reparations. In practice it was not really either of these things; but the misunderstanding of its true nature appears to have given a substantial fillip both to American isolationist thinking and to the Nazi Party in Germany.

The World Economic Conference took place in London in the summer of 1933. Everyone was suffering from the effects of international trade barriers, and most were too frightened to knock them down unilaterally. Some people, like the American Secretary of State, Cordell Hull, had high hopes for success of the Economic Conference; others, like the British Chancellor of the Exchequer, Neville Chamberlain, were much less sanguine. In the end the pessimists were proved right, and the Economic Conference collapsed.

The Disarmament Conference struggled on through these gloomy events. The final breakdown occurred in October 1933. The former Allies devised a sort of timetable which they proposed to the delegates. For four years after the conference ended, armaments should not be increased; then, over a further four-year period, there should be an agreed programme of reduction. Of course, these were merely proposals at this stage; but it was obvious that the conference would be likely to accept them.

The Germans declared that they had been cheated. During the first four-year phase, they would still be disarmed as a result of Versailles, while the other powers would not be disarming. With much drama and heat, Germany withdrew from the Disarmament Conference and also from the League of Nations.

In theory, the conference was still in being, though in suspended animation; in practice it was dead. If any one major power withdrew, it was meaningless for the others to remain at the conference table.

The effect was calamitous. If, after all these efforts, disarmament could not be agreed, then every nation must look to its own armaments to protect its interests, just as failure of the Economic Conference told the world that no general agreement could be expected on matters of trade. The League of Nations had already received a serious, perhaps a fatal, blow to its authority through the Sino-Japanese quarrel. The world had lurched into a period of international anarchy. It would be some time before the full implications of this state of affairs were generally appreciated; yet, almost immediately, people began to think not of disarmament but of rearmament.

Cartoon 11.1 Der französisch-tschechische Geheimvertrag. *Simplicissimus*, Munich, 7 April 1924

Der französisch-tschechische Geheimvertrag

Deutschland starrt wieder in Waffen.

'The Franco–Czech secret treaty' suggests that there was more in the Franco–Czech Treaty of January 1924 than was officially revealed. Be that as it may, the cartoon throws light on a common German attitude which developed soon after the war and continued for a long time.

The German digs his garden peacefully while tanks, guns, aeroplanes and bayonets from the neighbouring countries threaten his existence.

Cartoon 11.2 John Bull: 'Oh, mon cor . . .'. *Izvestiya,*
Moscow, copied by *L'Europe Nouvelle*, Paris,
1 December 1928

JOHN BULL : « Oh ! mon cor... »
[Lo point sensible · · le cor douloureux — c'est le désarmement naval.]

(Extrait des *Izvestia*, de Moscou.)

This is a Russian cartoon of 1928, commenting on the Anglo–French Naval Agreement of 1928 and American reactions to it. The incident which it commemorates was not, perhaps, of the first importance, but it provides a good object-lesson showing the kind of difficulties which faced people who, on the whole, were sincerely anxious to reach agreement about disarmament.

The Anglo–French Naval Agreement was to the effect that France should accept the British view that numbers of small cruisers should not be restricted, while Britain should accept the French view that the numbers of reserves should not be reckoned in limiting armies. Each country was, in effect, backing the other one's view of the armaments it regarded as necessary, in anticipation of the proposed Disarmament Conference.

In the previous year, there had been a Three-Power Conference, in which the third party was the United States. In response to American views, that conference had taken a different view of the small cruisers question. Many Americans were incensed by the new Anglo–French Naval Agreement, partly because it looked very much like an Anglo–French device to bypass themselves, and partly because the clause relating to cruisers was so phrased that it 'legalized' the small cruisers which Britain favoured, but not the large cruisers which suited the requirements of the United States. The American 'Note' of 28 September 1928, to which the Soviet cartoon alluded, was a formal complaint against the Anglo–French Agreement. John Bull's tender corn, on which Uncle Sam has just stamped, is labelled 'question of disarmament'.

The attitudes here attributed to Britain were very widespread. A country might well approve of disarmament in principle, but, when the proposed disarmament affected those elements which it considered of particular importance for the preservation of its own interests, then that country was likely to take a very different view. Furthermore, Britain and France were here cooperating to advance each other's interests, at the expense of other countries. The British, with their tiny army, had no interest in the question of army reserves which worried the French, while the French had no strong interest in the small cruisers which worried the British; but each country was backing the other in the matter. It is easy to see how similar attitudes and arrangements could become widespread among the nations, which would gravely weaken any prospect of serious disarmament.

In this German cartoon of 1931, whose title may be roughly translated 'The vulture of poverty brings Europa the palm of peace', Europa and the bull, in whose guise she was wooed by Zeus, are both starved as a result of the economic depression. The bird brings them, not food, but the palm-branch of peace. The implication is that universal poverty is likely to encourage nations to behave more peacefully towards each other, particularly in matters of armament limitation. Europa greets the bird with delight; the bull is less pleased.

Unfortunately, results were very different from those which the cartoon predicted. Within a short time of this cartoon appearing, Japan – impelled largely by poverty produced by the Depression – commenced her attack on China. Within a few months, the Nazis began to record spectacular advances in Germany.

186

Cartoon 11.3 Der Pleitegeier. *Simplicissimus*, Munich,
10 August 1931

Der Pleitegeier bringt Europa die Friedenspalme *(Th. Th. Heine)*

Cartoon 11.4 Passion 1932. *Simplicissimus*, Munich, 27 March 1932

This is a German cartoon for Easter 1932, commenting on the Disarmament Conference. It is a mark of the very real hopes which attended the inauguration of the conference.

The passion is not that of Christ, but of immense numbers of ordinary people who struggle to raise up the heavy cross. On the arms of the cross the statesmen of the world are seated; and the hope of the bearers of the cross is that they will succeed in their efforts.

Cartoon 11.5 Der amerikanische Abrüstungsvorschlag. *Simplicissimus*, Munich, 17 July 1932

This cartoon refers to an initiative by President Hoover of the United States, designed to help the Disarmament Conference out of the difficulties which it was encountering. In June 1932, the President proposed a general reduction of armaments by between 25 per cent and 33 per cent, and total abolition of certain kinds of weapons.

The European nations, all laden with armaments, are confronted with the American disarmament proposal. They reply in unison: 'It is easy for Hoover to talk, but, as long as we are not each twice as strong as our neighbour, we cannot think of disarmament.'

Cartoon 11.6 Tyazhely sluchai v Zheneve. *Pravda*, Moscow, 16 March 1933

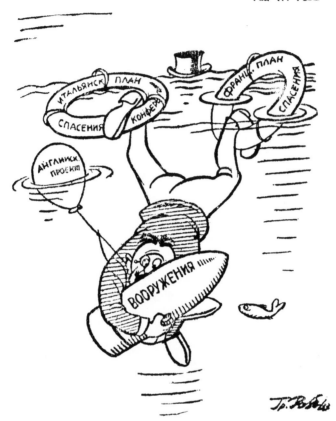

ТЯЖЕЛЫЙ СЛУЧАЙ В ЖЕНЕВЕ.

Рис. Гр. РОЗЕ.

«Он выплыть из всех напр... ...ется сил:
Но панцырь тяжелый его ·утопил».

(В. А. Жуковский).

These cartoons were drawn several months later, and express similar frustration at the lack of progress of the Disarmament Conference.

In the Soviet cartoon, 'Heavy going at Geneva', the conference clutches a great load of armaments, which are weighing it down in the water. The lifebelts, 'Italian plan for saving the conference' and 'French plan for saving' are of little help; nor is the balloon 'English project'. Statesmen cannot save the conference by clever verbal devices, but only by willingness to discard their cherished armaments.

Cartoon 11.7 Brilliant success of the conference so far.
Evening Standard, London, 22 June 1933

BRILLIANT SUCCESS OF THE CONFERENCE SO FAR. *(Copyright in all countries.)*

The British cartoon, ironically entitled 'Brilliant success of the conference so far', scarcely exaggerates the cause of the trouble, and is more or less self-explanatory. Even if the statesmen portrayed had had the vision to look beyond immediate perceived national interests towards the wider interests of all nations, they were all compelled by the exigencies of the intensely public debate to 'play to the gallery' and appeal to the crudest forms of domestic opinion.

Dr Dollfuss of Austria, who features in the middle of the illustration, was a very small man – 'the pocket Chancellor', he was sometimes called. His country, though also small, occupied a very important position in Europe.

Cartoon 11.8 Chaque chose en son temps. *L'Humanité*,
Paris, 12 February 1932

- La conférence de Genève entique-
t-elle notre intervention en Chine?
- Elle n'a pas le temps, Majesté, elle
s'occupe du désarmement.

'Everything in time' is the title of this French cartoon. The Japanese
Emperor asks a high officer whether the Geneva Conference is criticizing
Japanese intervention in Manchuria. The reply is that they have not the
time; they are busy with disarmament.

The Disarmament Conference had opened a little over a week before
the cartoon appeared. One of the considerations which probably influenced League of Nations countries in relation to the Manchurian question
was a fear that any very strong action against Japan might prejudice
success of the Disarmament Conference.

Cartoon 11.9 Le Beau Geste. *Evening Standard*, London, 11 March 1930

LE BEAU GESTE.

Cartoons 11.9, 11.10 and 11.11, which were drawn at considerable intervals, bring out the continuing character of the Franco-German dispute about 'security' and 'equality'.

The first cartoon, 'Le Beau Geste', appeared in 1930, almost two years before the Disarmament Conference began, and at a time when the Nazis formed an insignificant minority in the German Reichstag. There is a pun in the title; Beau Geste was a heroic fictional Englishman in the French Foreign Legion, while the words literally mean 'fine gesture'.

Briand, the French Foreign Minister, wears paper armour – i.e. the international engagements which apparently guaranteed French security: the Covenant of the League of Nations, the Locarno Pact and the Kellogg–Briand Pact. Behind him are massive guns, in front a submarine. He confronts other statesmen at the table of the future Disarmament Conference. The first one is probably Curtius, Foreign Minister of Germany, the second is Ramsay MacDonald, Prime Minister of Britain, the third is Grandi, Foreign Minister of Italy.

Briand's reference to the Foreign Legion is, of course, meant to be fatuous, although it fits in neatly with the title of the cartoon; but the

193

Cartoon 11.10 Equal harps for all. *Punch*, London,
5 October 1932

EQUAL HARPS FOR ALL.

Germany. " I WANT TO BE AN ANGEL AND PLAY AN INSTRUMENT OF PEACE. BUT
IF THEY WON'T LET ME HAVE ONE OF THE SAME SIZE AS THEIRS I SHALL GO
ON BEATING THIS."

Cartoon 11.11 Mariannes Papagei. *Simplicissimus*, Munich,
9 July 1933

Mariannes Papagei
Le perroquet de Marianne | Madame La France's Parrot | Il pappagallo di Marianna

real meaning of the cartoon is clearly indicated by the words at the bottom left. The British and German delegates are bemused. The Italian is more calm, but prepares to talk with Mussolini about possible changes in Italian foreign policy. The cartoonist seems to show irritation with the French attitude, and evidently thinks that France is already quite secure enough.

The second cartoon was drawn when the Disarmament Conference had already been in session for several months. In this cartoon, it appears that other countries may be willing to be 'angels' and 'play instruments of peace'. The German, however, is only prepared to join in the concert if he is allowed a harp of equal size to the others. If that is refused, he will play a much noisier and more discordant instrument.

The German cartoon, 'Marianne's parrot', lampoons the French demand for 'security'. France it implies, is already extremely heavily armed; but her constant cry for further 'security' makes all Europe insecure. When that cartoon was drawn, however, Hitler had already been in power for several months, and the French call for security was beginning to sound a good deal more reasonable than it had done three years earlier.

By the middle of 1932, economic conditions in Europe made it fairly evident that German reparations, and most Allied war debts, would not be paid for a very long time. A conference of European countries at Lausanne did not formally abrogate those various debts, but made arrangements from which it was clear that repayment at any time was most unlikely.

This caused considerable resentment in the United States. Uncle Sam views the skywriting on the European clouds – the clouds of the Depression – with visible disapproval. 'No more war' was a popular slogan at the time; but the extra word on the end did not please the Americans.

Cartoon 11.12 The writing on the clouds. *Punch*, London, 13 July 1932

THE WRITING ON THE CLOUDS.

UNCLE SAM. "SAY, THEY'VE WRITTEN A SKYFUL!"

[The Select Committee on Sky-writing has recently published a favourable report.]

Cartoon 11.13 The Downing Street nightingale. *Punch*, London, 17 May 1933

THE DOWNING STREET NIGHTINGALE.

Mr. Ramsay MacDonald (*slightly altering Milton*)—

"O NIGHTINGALE, THAT ON YON BLOOMY SPRAY
    WARBLEST AT EVE, WHEN ALL THE STREETS ARE STILL,
    THOU WITH FRESH HOPE A PREMIER'S HEART DOTH FILL."

Cartoon 11.13 was drawn at the beginning of the World Economic Conference. In spite of his various troubles – signalled by the books on his desk – MacDonald greets inauguration of the new conference in London with eager pleasure. The nightingale sings, as MacDonald spoke, with a Scottish accent.

Cartoon 11.14 MacDonalds letzte Bemühung. *Simplicissimus*, Munich, 6 August 1933

Mac Donalds letzte Bemühung

(Karl Arnold)

„. . . und erst vor sieben Wochen feierten sechsundsechzig Nationen den Tag seiner Geburt."

This cartoon, 'MacDonald's latest task', appeared in Germany a few months later, after the conference had collapsed. In miserable weather, MacDonald conveys the coffin of his infant 'Economic Conference' on the child's perambulator to the grave. He muses sadly, 'And seven weeks ago sixty-six nations were celebrating the day of his birth!'

199

Cartoon 11.15 Holding the baby. *Daily Express*, London, 17 October 1933

"HOLDING THE BABY"

This cartoon appeared just after Germany left the Disarmament Conference. The conference had in fact failed altogether in its purpose; but this was not yet quite clear. The proprietor of the *Daily Express*, in which the cartoon appeared, considered that Britain's main concern should be with her Empire, not with European quarrels.

The cartoon reflects on the last stage of the 'equality/security' debate between Germany and France. The two countries argue bitterly at 'Geneva Corner', while other nations look on. John Bull is 'holding the baby' of responsibilities incurred at Locarno eight years earlier. The 'little man', with whom the reader is really being asked to identify himself, points out to him that he is 'wanted on the Empire telephone' – in other words, that he has other responsibilities which concern him more closely than European rivalries.

The modern reader sometimes finds it hard to appreciate the size and international importance of the British Empire in those days. A great many Britons had relatives living there, particularly but by no means exclusively in the Dominions, and felt far more affinity with the Empire than with European countries – or, for that matter, with the League of Nations.

200

Cartoon 11.16 Er riechet schon! *Simplicissimus,* Munich, 10 December 1933

Er riechet schon!

(Wilhelm Schulz)

VÖLKERBUND

„Das einzige, was wir nicht vertagen können, ist die Beerdigung."

This is another German 'funeral' cartoon from the same magazine as Cartoon 11.14, though by a different artist. The coffin is inscribed 'League of Nations'; the title means 'He stinks already!' The mourner reflects,

'The one thing we can't postpone is the funeral.' There seems to be a reference to the raising of Lazarus (John 11, especially v. 39).

In one sense, the League of Nations was certainly not dead at the end of 1933, and it was to witness some very important and heated debates a couple of years later. Yet in another sense it was dead, and perhaps even 'stinking'. It had failed to take any effective action against Japan over Manchuria, and had more recently been flouted by the German announcement of withdrawal in October. Many people still entertained some desperate faith in its value; but that faith was more likely to mislead than to help them.

12

Setting the scene, 1933–4

The Great Depression hit different countries at different times; but in most places conditions were improving perceptibly by 1934. By that time, however, destabilization had gone too far for economic amelioration to halt the general drift towards anarchy and war. If an avalanche is started, it will continue even though the force which originally set it in motion has ceased to operate.

Events of 1933 and 1934 largely set the scene for the tragic occurrences which marked the later part of the decade. Some of these events have already been considered: Hitler's accession to office in Germany in January 1933; the collapse of the Disarmament Conference later in the same year; the failure of the League of Nations to exert control over Japanese aggression in Manchuria.

When Hitler became German Chancellor, his power was still far from complete. The Nazis only constituted one-fourth of his first Cabinet, which included formidable non-Nazi personalities like Hugenberg and von Papen. Hitler soon demanded, and obtained, a general election for 5 March 1933. That election was held in a deeply charged atmosphere. Not long before polling day, the Reichstag was destroyed by fire. A half-witted Dutch Communist was blamed, perhaps correctly. On the day of the fire, an Emergency Decree was issued, heavily curtailing the press and free speech.

Even so, the Nazis fell considerably short of an overall majority. Many elected deputies to the Reichstag who were opponents of the Nazis were proscribed, and the remainder soon gave the administration what amounted to complete power to run the country as it wished. Within a short time, all other political parties, and all organs of opinion of which the Nazis disapproved, were banned. Non-Nazis were gradually eased out of the government, while soon concentration camps and other instruments of terror were in full operation. The whole process was astonishingly short, and the resistance offered by the many victims astonishingly weak.

What happened in Germany was bound to affect Austria. When the Austro-Hungarian Empire collapsed, the German-speaking areas which today we call Austria were forbidden to unite with Germany. How many Austrians desired this *Anschluss* at various dates, it is impossible to say.

In 1931, an attempt was made by the German and Austrian governments to achieve a *Zollverein*, or customs union, between the two countries. This was one of the few examples of countries seeking to liberalize rather than to restrict trade in response to the Depression. Whether the proposed arrangement was technically legal or not under various international engagements was never convincingly determined; but great financial pressure was exerted from France to destroy it. As a result, the principal Austrian bank, Kreditanstalt, fell into great difficulties, with many side-effects on the Austrian economy. Thus Austria suffered particularly badly from the general economic depression of the period.

Early in 1934, there was virtual civil war in Vienna, and considerable trouble in other important Austrian cities. The Austrian government was backed by the more or less Fascist 'paramilitary' Heimwehr; their principal opponents were an extreme Socialist group, the Schutzbund.

The summer of 1934 provided some grave warnings as to the character of Nazism in both Germany and Austria. On 30 June, the 'night of the long knives', Hitler's leading rivals within the Nazi Party itself, and a number of other individuals with whom he had quarrelled, were murdered. Less than a month later, Austrian Nazis murdered the country's Chancellor, Engelbert Dollfuss.

It is striking to note that Mussolini promptly moved Italian troops to the Austrian frontier, with the object of forestalling, not assisting, a German takeover. Relations between the two dictators were by no means good at this stage. Austria was more or less an Italian protégé. Mussolini had no wish to lose it to Germany, while he also had good reason to fear that a united 'Greater Germany' might lay claim to former Austro-Hungarian territory which Italy had taken after 1918.

The international excitement which followed the murder of Dollfuss was considerable. Hitler was able to turn it to good account, by removing the German ambassador in Vienna, who was to some extent implicated in the aftermath of the crime, and replacing him with von Papen – thus removing one of the few remaining forces of moderation in his own government.

A few days after the murder of Dollfuss, President von Hindenburg died. This death was apparently due to natural causes; but it could hardly have come at a more convenient moment for Hitler. Public attention was immediately deflected, while Hitler took the occasion to assume the office of President as well as that of Chancellor.

While Hitler was consolidating power in Germany, France was experiencing troubles of many kinds. The Depression hit France rather later than most countries. In 1932, the country's political stability began to crumble, a state of affairs which may be attributed in part to economic causes and in part to the accident of a particularly indecisive general election. The same year saw the death of Aristide Briand. At the turn of 1933–4, the Stavisky scandal revealed the personal corruption of a number of the country's leading statesmen belonging to the 'moderate left', and raised doubts about the probity of others.

Not long afterwards, a more 'right-wing' government was set up, under Gaston Doumergue. That government depended largely on the personality of the Foreign Minister, Louis Barthou; but Barthou was assassinated at Marseille in October, along with King Alexander of Yugoslavia. Doumergue resigned not long afterwards, and a succession of short-lived governments followed. Barthou's own successor as Foreign Minister was Pierre Laval. Laval would eventually die at the end of the Second World War in front of a firing squad, as a collaborator with the Germans.

While France's internal politics were in this parlous condition, her foreign relations encountered difficulties of their own. Early in 1934, Poland and Germany concluded a non-aggression pact. This new arrangement may or may not have been incompatible with the words of the Franco–Polish Mutual Assistance Agreement reached at Locarno; but it was certainly incompatible with the spirit. France now had good reason for doubting whether Poland could be considered a reliable ally in case of trouble. Alexander's assassination cast similar doubts about one of France's strongest allies in eastern Europe, for the King was the real as well as the titular head of his country.

In these circumstances, French foreign policy was apparently free to move in several radically different directions. A serious effort might be made to contain the new, and much more serious, German threat by international alliances. If so, then who should those allies be? Different potential allies might have interests which conflicted with those both of each other and of France. Or France might despair of allies, and look to her own security, by building strong defence forces, and particularly frontier defences. Or France might decide that Germany was in the long run invincible, and try to reach what terms she could. In the ensuing years, all of these courses had their advocates, and it was quite possible for a person to swing very suddenly from favouring one course to favouring a very different one.

Choices in some ways similar to those confronting France were facing the Soviet Union. In the 1920s and early 1930s, she had regarded all 'capitalist' countries as enemies, while the League of Nations was seen as, at best, ineffectual and, at worst, a kind of robbers' conspiracy.

Soon after Hitler consolidated power in Germany, a great change took place in Soviet diplomatic thinking. During the period of Hitler's rise to power, the Soviet authorities seem to have thought that a Nazi Government in Germany was not necessarily a bad thing, for the experience would drive German workers rapidly towards Communism. Soon after Hitler took power, it became apparent that this development was not likely to occur in the near future, if at all. On the other hand, the Nazis made no secret of huge territorial designs on the Soviet Union, and were rapidly preparing to execute those designs. Thus a dramatic change in

Soviet policy became necessary. That change was marked symbolically by the appointment of Maxim Litvinov as Commissar for Foreign Affairs. The Soviet Union soon joined the League of Nations, and showed considerable eagerness to cooperate with other countries against the German threat.

Cartoon 12.1 13 Jahre Verelendungspolitik. *Völkischer Beobachter*, Munich, 2 February 1933

13 Jahre Verelendungspolitik

Der Angeklagte kann vortreten - - -

This is a Nazi cartoon which appeared just after Hitler took office as Chancellor. The title may be translated roughly as '13 years of politics of misery'. The cartoon alludes to the Nazi argument that the 'Marxists' – a generic word which included both Communists and Social Democrats – were responsible for most of Germany's troubles in the period.

The German people are in the seat of judgement, and 'Marxism' is the defendant. The charge-sheet begins with 'November [19]18' – for the Nazi myth held that the 'Marxists' had brought about Germany's collapse by subversion. It goes on with reference to 'Versailles' – for the German 'Marxists' were blamed for accepting a 'shameful' peace treaty. It continues with 'Dawes' and 'Young', implying that the 'Marxists' were at fault for acknowledging the existence of a German 'war debt' when they concluded these arrangements. The words at the bottom mean 'The accused may step forward.'

Cartoon 12.2 'Happy days are here again!'. *Daily Express*, London, 2 February 1933

"HAPPY DAYS ARE HERE AGAIN"

These British cartoons, also drawn just after Hitler took office, show apprehensions and misapprehensions about the nature and intentions of the Nazis.

In the first cartoon, the ex-Kaiser and his son, the former Crown Prince ('Little Willie', as he was commonly known in Britain during the war), rejoice at the news of Hitler's accession to office. They are preparing uniforms and regalia in anticipation of an early restoration of the Hohenzollern monarchy. The ex-Kaiser seems to be wearing Dutch trousers and clogs, for he was currently in exile in the Netherlands. His son, whose sympathy for the Nazis was more blatant than that of his father, is wearing a swastika. The song, 'Happy days are here again', was very popular in the period. In the top right of the cartoon is a picture of the ex-Kaiser in the days of his glory. Whatever the two men may have thought of the prospects of a Hohenzollern restoration, Hitler had no intention of sharing power with them, or with anybody else.

Cartoon 12.3 'Let the German people decide!'. *Evening Standard*, London, 1 March 1933

"LET THE GERMAN PEOPLE DECIDE !"

(Copyright in all countries.)

The second cartoon shows Hitler in the pocket of a smiling figure who carries the word 'Reaction' on his lapel. The face of 'Reaction' is similar to that of the German Nationalist leader Hugenberg, who was included in Hitler's first Cabinet. Hugenberg could perhaps be termed, loosely, a 'reactionary', but Hitler had ideas based on a frightening vision of the future rather than any kind of hankering for the past. Perhaps Hugenberg and those like him thought that they were 'using' Hitler; in fact Hitler was using them.

The cartoon appeared at the time of the German general election. The polling booth in the background is guarded by armed men, who plainly intend to terrorize anybody wishing to vote the 'wrong' way. This cartoon received the unusual 'compliment' of being copied in the Soviet newspaper *Pravda* (7 March 1933), with the wording translated into Russian.

Cartoon 12.4 The red peril. *Punch*, London, 8 March 1933

THE RED PERIL.

The Old Consul (*to Hitler*). "THIS IS A HEAVEN-SENT OPPORTUNITY, MY LAD.
IF YOU CAN'T BE A DICTATOR NOW, YOU NEVER WILL BE."

This British cartoon appeared shortly after the Reichstag fire of 28 February 1933, and the grant of emergency powers to Hitler which followed later on the same day. The burning Reichstag is in the background. President Hindenburg, 'the old Consul', hands over these special powers to Hitler, the new 'Dictator'.

The office of 'Dictator' originated in the Roman republic, and was granted for a limited period in times of extreme emergency: hence the Roman dress and titles in the cartoon. Readers of *Punch* in that period would probably have been a good deal more familiar with allusions to Roman antiquity than would be their modern successors.

The implication of the cartoon seems to be that the Reichstag fire was indicative of a real and deep-seated 'red peril', rather than the action of an unbalanced individual acting on his own – which is now the general view of the incident. The cartoonist seems to approve of the action which Hindenburg and Hitler were taking. Many people in Britain and other countries, who would certainly not rank as 'pro-Nazis' in the ordinary sense of the term, were by no means hostile to Hitler in the earliest days of his rule.

Cartoon 12.5 Trödelmarkt. *Simplicissimus*, Munich, 21 May 1933

Trödelmarkt

"Dös san die neuesten Antiquitäten, sicherns Eahna a Stück!"

This cartoon appeared in *Simplicissimus* in May 1933. Before Hitler established effective control, this periodical had often been very critical of the Nazis, but by the date of this cartoon it may be regarded as entirely pro-Nazi in its sympathies. Indeed, the German authorities would not have permitted it to continue publication otherwise.

The cartoon alludes to the rapid collapse of the non-Nazi political parties. The customers are being offered the Communist symbol in a junk-shop, which also displays emblems of other political parties. It implies that those parties have already become things of the past – 'most recent antiques – make sure you get one', the saleswoman is saying. The Nazi suppression of other German parties was still not quite complete when this cartoon appeared, but within a month or so they had ceased to exist.

Cartoon 12.6 Springtime in Europe. *Evening Standard*, London, 28 March 1931

AUSTRIA: "But didn't you ask us all to love one another?"
BRIAND: "Oui, mes enfants — but not in the manner so exclusive."

SPRINGTIME IN EUROPE.

(*Copyright in all countries.*)

This cartoon was drawn in March 1931 – a couple of years before Cartoon 12.5 – and comments on the German–Austrian *Zollverein* (customs union) plan, which had recently been published. The idea was to remove customs barriers between the two countries but maintain common tariffs towards the outside world.

The French Foreign Minister Briand, as Cupid, confronts the lovers Germany (represented by Chancellor Brüning) and Austria. 'Cupid' admits that he has 'asked us all to love one another' – that is, he has advocated strongly the idea of a 'United States of Europe', which would necessarily involve a general removal of customs barriers by the European countries, but objects to the 'exclusive' character of the German–Austrian relationship.

Briand's retinue are Arthur Henderson, British Foreign Minister in the 1929–31 Labour Government, the Italian Foreign Minister Grandi, and a representative of Czechoslovakia – perhaps Prime Minister Malypetr, but certainly not the beardless Foreign Minister Beneš.

The *Zollverein* proposals produced angry French reactions, because of the fear that a German–Austrian bloc would prove too powerful an economic unit. Czechoslovakia had good reasons to fear such an arrangement because of its geographical location, while Italy looked upon Austria as something of a satellite. Britain, who had less to fear from a German economic recovery, was disposed – despite the cartoon – to play a much cooler part.

―――――――――――――

'Rescue Austria quickly' is the legend at the top of this German cartoon of June 1931. French financiers – with or without government prompting – were exerting enormous economic pressure, which was having disastrous effects on the extremely important Austrian bank Kreditanstalt.

In this cartoon, Vienna has almost disappeared between the waters, leaving only the spire of St Stephen's Cathedral protruding, while Austrian bankers on the wreckage of Kreditanstalt are reaching for a lifebelt. The French were offering to 'save' Kreditanstalt on very onerous terms, while the British were attempting to offer a financial rescue operation.

The Austrian bankers conclude that, when all goes well, there should be no interference with the private economy; but that there is no objection to nationalization of a bankrupt institution.

Cartoon 12.7 S(taniert) O(esterreich) S(chnell).
Simplicissimus, Munich, 22 June 1931

Cartoon 12.8 Dollfussland. *Simplicissimus*, Munich, 4 March 1934

Statt einer Volksabstimmung!

Austria's economic troubles led to profound political troubles, and the Austrian Chancellor Dollfuss was at the centre of these troubles. 'Dollfuss-land' is a bitter Nazi comment on the near-civil war of February 1934. The 'result of an election' – i.e. instead of a plebiscite – is seen in corpses lying on the Viennese street. There was a considerable amount of fighting between Austrian government forces and the revolutionary Socialist Schutzbund.

The Austrian Nazis more or less stood aside while the fighting went on, but the burden of this cartoon is to suggest that the whole sequence of events was due to the politics of Dollfuss. The Chancellor was murdered by Austrian Nazis a few months later.

Cartoon 12.9 A friend of peace. *Punch*, London,
27 January 1932

A FRIEND OF PEACE.

MADAME LA RÉPUBLIQUE. "IF YOU MUST GO, M. BRIAND, FAREWELL; AND MAY
YOU SOON BE RESTORED TO THE SERVICE OF MANKIND!"

M. BRIAND. "THANK YOU FOR YOUR GOOD WISHES, MADAME. I COUNT ON YOU
DURING MY ABSENCE TO TAKE CHARGE OF THIS, MY CONSTANT COMPANION OF
RECENT YEARS."

This cartoon commemorates the departure from office of Aristide Briand.
Briand did not return, as Marianne had hoped; he died a few weeks later.
After Briand, it became increasingly difficult for France to formulate any
consistent foreign policy. As the whole climate of world politics was
deteriorating rapidly, this was a most serious loss.

Cartoon 12.10 Frankreichs Aussen- und Innenpolitik. Simplicissimus, Munich, 4 March 1934

Frankreichs Außen- und Innenpolitik

(E. Schilling)

Ist im Staate etwas faul,
herrscht nach außen hin das Maul.

The German cartoon, 'French foreign and domestic politics' (Cartoon 12.10), was drawn at a time when Hitler had already been in office for a year. Louis Barthou, who had recently become French Foreign Minister, showed signs of concern, which were interpreted in Germany as provocative. Louis Barthou was the sort of man to encourage that assessment.

The cartoonist links Barthou's international attitude with the Stavisky scandal which broke a few weeks earlier, and which gravely weakened the reputations of a considerable number of French politicians. He suggests that the chaos of French internal politics and 'something rotten in the state' was encouraging France to pursue a chauvinistic foreign policy.

This cartoon alludes to the German–Polish Non-aggression Pact of January 1934. The 'sensation in Geneva' is the dove of peace, which carries the German emblem on one wing and the Polish emblem on the other. The Allied diplomats are astonished at the 'peace pact' as they have neither initiated it nor prevented it.

The pact was a remarkable diplomatic achievement for the Germans, for it seriously undermined French foreign policy, and cast doubts on the continued validity of the Franco–Polish Mutual Assistance Agreement concluded at Locarno. If the Germans had honoured the agreement (which they did not), it would have been equally beneficial for Poland, which lived in constant dread of renewed German claims to the 'Polish Corridor' established at Versailles.

Cartoon 12.11 Sensation in Genf. *Simplicissimus*, Munich. 18 February 1934

„Eine deutsch-polnische Friedenstaube? — Und wir haben es weder veranlasst noch verhindern können."

Cartoon 12.12 The sudden squall. *Evening Standard*,
London, 12 October 1934

THE SUDDEN SQUALL   *(Copyright in All Countries)*

'The sudden squall' commemorated in this cartoon was the assassination
of Louis Barthou, French Foreign Minister, and King Alexander of Yugoslavia by a Croat nationalist at Marseille, on 9 October 1934.

Barthou had been far from popular with other diplomats – including
British diplomats – during his period of office, but there could be little
question that he was successfully asserting French influence, and when he
died his policy largely collapsed. So, too, did the French government of
which he had been a leading member.

King Alexander had taken a strongly pro-French line, and the 'Little
Entente' of Yugoslavia, Romania and Czechoslovakia was a major factor
in the politics of eastern Europe. After Alexander's death, his young son
became King, but there was necessarily a long regency in which it was
by no means clear what direction Yugoslavia would take.

Cartoon 12.13 Sowjetdiplomatie. *Simplicissimus*, Munich, 6 October 1935

Herr Litwinow macht in Genf in Pazifismus | Herr Litwinow sorgt in Moskau für die Weltrevolution.

The arrival, and consolidation, of Nazism in Germany produced deep changes in Soviet diplomacy. In the course of 1934, the Soviet Union joined the League of Nations, which it had formerly despised, and soon tried to establish itself as the nucleus of international resistance to Nazi Germany.

The question which concerned a great many people was whether this marked a real change in foreign policy in the sense that the old 'Comintern' idea of using the Soviet Union as the basis of 'world revolution' had been finally abandoned, or whether it was no more than a reaction of fear to the threat which Nazi Germany posed to the USSR, which included a desire to embroil others with Germany in the hope that Russia could escape trouble.

The Nazis, of course, had every reason for encouraging the view that the Soviet 'conversion' was thoroughly insincere. In the cartoon of 1935 on the previous page, 'Soviet diplomacy', one half of Maxim Litvinov, Soviet Commissar for Foreign Affairs, pleads at Geneva for peace, while the other half calls in Moscow for world revolution.

13

The end of the old order, 1935

On 16 March 1935, Hitler announced that Germany would no longer be bound by the disarmament clauses of the Treaty of Versailles – specifically, that she would introduce conscription and establish an air force.

The three major Allied powers in Europe were Britain, France and Italy. On 11 April, the three heads of government – MacDonald, Flandin and Mussolini – and their Foreign Ministers met at Stresa in Italy. After a few days' deliberation, they made a number of statements. By far the most important of these was a declaration that they would not favour a German move into Austria.

Why did it take such a high-powered conference to make such a simple announcement? Why did the three powers, all of whom were threatened in various ways by Hitler's earlier declaration, not agree to something much more impressive – an announcement, for example, that they proposed to occupy Germany by military force unless the Führer immediately retracted what he had said earlier? The answer to the question seems to be that all three Allies had what we might call reserve options in mind.

The French government was contemplating a mutual assistance agreement with the Soviet Union, and commenced negotiations shortly after Stresa, although the agreement was not formally concluded until the following year. The idea was that if either country were attacked by Germany, the other would go to its assistance.

Yet how, we may ask, could Germany attack the Soviet Union, with which she had no common frontier? Or, for that matter, how could the Soviet Union go to the aid of France, if France were the victim? Poland must be involved in both cases, either as an ally or as an enemy, to make the arrangement effective. The Franco–Soviet agreement could hardly fail to affect and embarrass both Britain and Italy, to say nothing of Poland.

The British government had other ideas in mind. In June, an agreement was reached with Germany, affecting their respective naval armaments. Under this agreement, Germany agreed to keep her navy down to roughly 35 per cent of the British. The trouble with the arrangement was that Germany was already required, under Versailles, to keep her navy down to a much smaller size than that. Indeed, the naval clauses of Versailles had not been repudiated by Hitler's March announcement. By making the new agreement, Britain was in effect condoning a major breach of Versailles, to the embarrassment of France and Italy.

The Italian government had other plans, which will require fuller discussion in the next chapter.

Cartoon 13.1 Cause precedes effect. *Evening Standard,* London, 20 March 1935

CAUSE PRECEDES EFFECT   (Copyright in All Countries)

This cartoon was drawn shortly after Hitler's announcement of 16 March 1935, that Germany was going to rearm.

Hitler takes the salute. The soldiers in the rear of the marching column are Germans, who would be expected to salute the Führer. The statesmen in the front, however, are people who would thoroughly disapprove of the announcement, but whom the cartoonist is disposed to blame, to a greater or lesser extent, for what has happened.

Heading the file are the ghosts of Clémenceau, carrying the Versailles Treaty, and Marshal Foch. Behind them march the ghosts of Poincaré, apparently Lloyd George (although he was still alive at the time of the cartoon) and Lord Curzon, who was Foreign Secretary in the latter part of the Coalition period. Between the ghosts and the soldiers are (from left to right) Laval, Mussolini, Sir John Simon, MacDonald (still British Prime Minister at this date) and Sir Austen Chamberlain.

Some of the statesmen, living and dead, had long been targets of the pungent criticism of cartoonist Low; but in other cases it is difficult to see on what ground they are being blamed for the recent developments.

227

Cartoon 13.2 Der Blinde. *Simplicissimus*, Munich, 16 September 1934

„. . . ‚der Krieg ist die höchste gerichtliche Instanz zwischen den Völkern. Man muß also für den Krieg bereit sein, nicht für morgen, sondern schon für heute!'" — „Maledetto! Diese Barbaren von Deutschen!" — „No, no, padre: das hat der Duce gesagt."

'The blind man' is a German cartoon from September 1934, and serves as a reminder of the bitter relations which existed between Mussolini's Italy and Hitler's Germany in the early days of Nazi rule.

The young Italian in the background is reading a newspaper. The blind man, who also has only one leg, is perhaps visualized as a victim of the war. The reader quotes, 'War is the highest way of deciding [i.e. the highest court of appeal] between nations. We must therefore be ready for war, not for some time or other, but for today!'

The blind man, who misunderstands the source of the quotation, is horrified. 'Shocking! These German barbarians!' The young man replies. 'No, no, dad, that's what the Duce [i.e. Mussolini] said!'

In this period, Mussolini sometimes made warlike speeches although this particular quotation, probably based on his Bologna speech of August 1934, is rather out of context. Yet such speeches were very disturbing, and go a considerable way towards explaining why British and French politicians were disposed to keep Mussolini at arm's length, and not cooperate too closely with him in resisting Nazi Germany.

Cartoon 13.3 Delicate progress. *Evening Standard*, London, 10 April 1935

DELICATE PROGRESS.

(Copyright in All Countries)

This cartoon, drawn just before the Stresa Conference, shows how the pattern of international politics appeared in the early spring of 1935, and may be contrasted sharply with the way matters looked a few months later.

Sir John Simon, British Foreign Secretary, treads the fence, with 'British foreign policy' as his balancing-rod. On one side of the fence are Hitler and a representative of Japan. This was not a surprising combination, for the two countries were moving rapidly towards an alliance, which was signalled in the 'Anti-Comintern Pact' of November 1936.

Much more remarkable, however, are the three men on the other side: Laval, Mussolini and Stalin. Laval and Mussolini were among the instigators of the Stresa Conference, which Simon also attended; but the attitudes which the two men took were very different, for Mussolini was then much the stronger supporter of a vigorous line against Hitler. All three of them were destined, at one time or another, to cooperate with Hitler far more closely than Simon wished to do; and two of them would eventually pay with their lives for that cooperation.

The rapidly changing pattern of alliances and animosities during the middle and later 1930s made it inordinately difficult for any British statesman to chart a clear course.

230

Cartoon 13.4 This year's problem picture. *Daily Express*, London, 11 April 1935

THIS YEAR'S PROBLEM PICTURE

This is a Strube cartoon linking the Stresa discussions with the considerable public interest excited by the annual Royal Academy exhibition.

The Allied statesmen – MacDonald and Simon of Britain, Laval and Flandin of France, Mussolini of Italy – are drawn as art critics, discussing the paradoxical 'problem picture' displayed. Hitler is portrayed as a benevolent and peaceful angel; yet the frame of the picture is made from shells and gasmasks. Which is the 'real' character of Nazi Germany: a peaceful country, desiring no more than equality with everybody else; or a menace to peace, whose recent rearmament announcement threatened everybody? There was much honest doubt on the subject in the spring of 1935, just as there was also doubt as to what kind of action should be taken if the more gloomy view should prove correct.

Cartoon 13.5 Overdue repairs. *News of the World*, London, 26 May 1935

OVERDUE REPAIRS.

JOHN BULL (to Mr. Baldwin): " That's the way, Stan ! I was beginning to feel a draught ! "

Mr. Baldwin announced in the House of Commons the measures to be taken for the expansion of the Royal Air Force.

Stanley Baldwin – not yet Prime Minister, but already the 'strong man' of the National Government – mends the British roof with tiles marked 'air defence', to the approval of John Bull, while the storm cloud 'air menace' carries the faces of Hitler and (probably) his Air Minister, Goering.

The Germans had recently announced their intention to build a strong air force. In this period, nobody was very sure just how serious the threat of air bombardment would be, but many people were appalled at the danger. The British government was moving slowly towards rearmament, particularly in the air, but was encountering strong criticism from political opponents in the Labour Party (but not in the Liberal Party) for so doing.

Cartoon 13.6 Ein Tor gewonnen! *Simplicissimus*, Munich, 7 July 1935

Ein Tor gewonnen!

Bravo! Nur so weiter! Bravo!

This German cartoon, 'One goal scored!' commemorates the Anglo–German Naval Agreement of June 1935.

Peace, with her palm-branch, kicks the ball 'German–English Naval Agreement' into the goal, supported by players wearing German and British insignia. Mars and Marianne have both been frustrated in their efforts to prevent the goal. 'Hurrah! That's the way to go on!' is the comment.

The Anglo–German Naval Agreement, which authorized Germany to build up to about 35 per cent of Britain's naval strength, was hailed in Germany as a victory not just for German diplomacy but for peace. As Cartoon 13.5 showed, however, Britain was not relying exclusively on diplomacy, but was also beginning to rearm.

Cartoon 13.7 Another reunion. *Daily Herald*, London, 26 June 1935

Another Reunion of Enemy Ex-Service Men
(Or " Sh! Don't tell Parliament ")

This British 'opposition' cartoon takes a very different view of the Anglo–German Naval Agreement. British admirals are seen as conspirators, whose common interest with their German counterparts transcends their duty to their country.

The cartoon also reflects on the rather curious nature of the agreement. It was not a treaty in the ordinary sense, but an exchange of 'Notes' between the recently appointed British Foreign Secretary Sir Samuel Hoare and his German counterpart Joachim von Ribbentrop.

234

Cartoon 13.8 Marianne. *Simplicissimus*, Munich, 14 April 1935

Marianne

„Ihren Arm, Iwan! Man hat es gewagt, mich vor ein fait accompli zu stellen!"

This German cartoon appeared during the Stresa Conference. It was already known that France was contemplating some kind of agreement with the Soviet Union.

Marianne offers to take the arm of the Russian 'Ivan', because 'someone had had the impertinence to present me with a *fait accompli'*.

As these negotiations proceeded, many bitter cartoons appeared in Germany, savagely criticizing the projected French association with the Soviet Union, which was represented as a great threat to peace.

14

Abyssinia, 1935–6

Even before the Stresa Conference of April 1935, there were indications that the Italian government had some sort of designs on Abyssinia – or, as it is now known, Ethiopia. We may speculate as to how far the eventual attack was planned at that stage, and how much of this was a reaction to the very limited achievements at Stresa, and concern to prove to Germany that Italy was a strong power with whose interests it would be unwise to tamper.

Italy had two east African colonies, Italian Somaliland and Eritrea, which bordered Abyssinia. During the spring and summer of 1935, Italian warlike preparations developed, although several attempts were made to secure a compromise arrangement between the two countries. No attack could be made with any hope of success until the end of the rainy season. When the attack came, on 2 October, nobody was taken by surprise.

The League of Nations promptly condemned the Italian aggression, and soon began to apply a policy of economic sanctions against Italy. Sanctions, however, were always somewhat half-hearted, and the oil sanctions which might have been effective against the Italian operations were never applied.

The roles of Britain and France were of critical importance, for they were acknowledged great powers, with enormous overseas possessions and interests, but they were also the leading members of the League of Nations. The two governments deplored the Italian attack, and agreed to support sanctions; but they did not see matters in an identical light. On the whole, the British were more disposed to favour a strong line, even though the Cabinet reacted rather nervously when naval advisers pointed out the danger of a surprise Italian attack in the Mediterranean. The French were more inclined to drag their feet – not out of sympathy with Mussolini or fear of Italian counter-measures, but because they were anxious not to antagonize Italy too deeply, lest she be driven into the arms of Germany.

A curious and belated attempt at compromise was made in December 1935 – the so-called 'Hoare–Laval Pact', whose eponymous authors were the Foreign Ministers of Britain and France. The proposed arrangement, which never went so far as receiving official approval, failed on every count. Both belligerents rejected the ideas contained, and both of the authors were driven from office in their respective countries. The war continued; but in May 1936 the Italian victory was complete, and the King of Italy was proclaimed Emperor of Abyssinia.

From the point of view of Britain and France, the Italo–Abyssinian war was in every sense a disaster. Any war anywhere necessarily led to general instability, and from instability they had nothing to gain and everything to lose. The League of Nations, which they had supported as the principal instrument of international stability, was shown to be ineffective in circumstances far sharper and more convincing than the Manchurian incident of 1931–2. Towards Italy, they had proved themselves 'willing to wound but afraid to strike'. Thus they attracted both the ill-will and the contempt of Mussolini, who was driven, with some reluctance, to the conclusion that his best course was to secure accommodation with Hitler's Germany.

Cartoon 14.1 Another scrap of paper. *New York Herald-Tribune*, 4 October 1935

The contemptuous description of an international treaty as a 'scrap of paper' was originally attributed to the German Chancellor Bethmann Hollweg, and the view of international engagements which it epitomized was bitterly condemned in Allied countries during the First World War.

This American cartoon, which appeared at the beginning of the Italian invasion of Abyssinia, shows the 'World War lesson' as a 'scrap of paper' which lies torn and neglected by the roadside, close to a war cemetery, while detonations of the 'Ethiopian war' are seen in the distance.

The message is partly a moral one: that Italy has acted in defiance of her international engagements. It is partly a practical one: that Italy's refusal to heed the 'World War lesson' brings a much greater war perceptibly closer.

Cartoon 14.2 Da quale pulpito. *Il Popolo d'Italia*, Milan, 18 October 1935

Da quale pulpito viene la predica!

These three cartoons appeared in Mussolini's own newspaper, *Il Popolo d'Italia*. They indicate some of the arguments which the Italian government set before its own people in support of the aggression against Abyssinia.

The first cartoon, 'From what pulpit does the sermon come?' shows Italy and her children at their frugal table. From afar, John Bull, gluttonously devouring a great slice of the world, hypocritically admonishes them. If it was permissible for Britain (and France, for that matter) to acquire their enormous empires in the past, then what right had they to condemn Italy for doing the same thing on a much more modest scale?

The second cartoon, 'The aggressor and the victim', shows an Italian soldier, who has struck off the chains of an Abyssinian, now offering his 'victim' a portion of his own food. At this time, the Italian Fascists had not displayed the 'racist' ideology of the Nazis, and the Abyssinian is represented as an equal, not as an inferior. The broken chains on the Abyssinian's wrists may allude to the chattel-slavery which still existed in Abyssinia. Soon after this cartoon was drawn, however, the Italian invaders began to act in a barbaric manner toward the Abyssinians, sometimes bombarding them with poison gas.

The third cartoon, 'The salute of the Allied arms', is a bitter comment on the response of Italy's wartime allies to her current behaviour in

Cartoon 14.3 'L'aggressore e l'aggredito'. *Il Popolo d'Italia,*
Milan, 22 October 1935

Cartoon 14.4 Il saluto. *Il Popolo d'Italia,* Milan,
5 December 1935

Abyssinia. When Italy intervened in the First World War in 1915, she did so in response to the pressing invitation of Britain and France (in circumstances, incidentally, which reflect little credit on any of the three countries). The Allies greeted the Italian declaration of war with enthusiasm – hence the bayonets held in military salute. The same Allies, twenty years later, point their bayonets against Italy's body. 'Intervento' – intervention – of 1915 is contrasted with 'sanzioni' – sanctions – of 1935.

The figure 'XIV' in the second frame of the picture signifies 'the 14th year of the Fascist era'. Fascists sometimes used that form of dating, just as the first French Republic had dated its documents, coins, etc. from its own foundation.

This cartoon comments on the so-called 'Hoare–Laval Pact' of December 1935.

British Foreign Secretary Sir Samuel Hoare was passing through Paris on his way to a holiday in Switzerland, and for that part of the journey was accompanied by Sir Robert Vansittart, Civil Service head of the Foreign Office and a most trenchant critic of Nazi Germany. In Paris they met Hoare's French counterpart, Pierre Laval, and some discussions took place about a possible compromise solution to the Italo–Abyssinian war, based on a series of territorial exchanges in east Africa involving Britain, Italy and Abyssinia. These discussions, which had not been approved by either government, were leaked to the French press, and a great furore arose. It was argued that, under these proposals, Italy would be deriving some benefit – though not all that she had sought – from her aggression against Abyssinia.

Shortly after his arrival in Switzerland, Hoare had a painful accident, and was unable to explain his own position to the British Cabinet. Critics suspected the worst, and eventually both Hoare and Laval were forced to resign. It now seems likely that the main object of the proposals had been to avert a damaging and protracted dispute with Italy, from which Nazi Germany would be the ultimate beneficiary.

In the cartoon, Mussolini is asleep, his bed littered with newspapers carrying adverse reports of Italy's progress in the Abyssinian war. Above his bed, and underneath a bust of Mussolini arrayed as a Roman emperor, are pejorative slogans. Laval, as Father Christmas, delivers the Abyssinian Emperor Haile Selassie bound into Mussolini's stocking. Hoare and Anthony Eden (at that time Minister for League of Nations Affairs) are the reindeer pulling Father Christmas's sledge, whose load includes the bound League of Nations and oil for the prosecution of Mussolini's war.

242

Cartoon 14.5 Santa Claus comes to Mussolini. *Evening Standard*, London, 13 December 1935

The cartoon was based on an assessment of events which seemed reasonable at the time, but which must be qualified considerably in the light of modern knowledge. Mussolini's reverses are exaggerated, and, under the plan, Haile Selassie was to retain strictly Abyssinian parts of his empire. Eden, who was an exceptionally bitter opponent of Mussolini, certainly cannot be regarded as one of the 'reindeer'. Hoare's expression of bewilderment is appropriate; he had almost certainly been duped by the over-subtle Laval.

Cartoon 14.6 Finale. *Simplicissimus*, Munich, 24 May 1936

This German cartoon comments on the end of the Abyssinian war in May 1936.

The senile League of Nations receives news of events from a gloating victor. 'I am sorry to disturb your sleep, but I should like to tell you that you need no longer bother yourself about the Abyssinian business; the matter has been settled elsewhere.'

244

The Nazis had little direct interest in the outcome of the Abyssinian war. The victory of Mussolini was a tremendous blow to Britain and France, and effectively destroyed the League of Nations; but defeat for Mussolini would have removed a rival to German interests in central Europe.

Cartoon 14.7 In the melting pot again. *Evening Standard,* London, 6 May 1936

IN THE MELTING POT AGAIN.   *(Copyright in All Countries)*

This gloomy and prophetic cartoon was drawn shortly after the Italian victory. International agreements, the 'world's foreign policies' and the world's armaments are all 'in the melting pot again', heated by the flames of the Abyssinian capital. Addis Ababa was occupied by the Italians early in May 1936, but was not (as the cartoon rather suggests) put to the flames. The recipe book in the belt of the diabolical chef was accurately labelled.

Cartoon 14.8 'The confusion of tongues'. *Daily Express*, London, 21 October 1936

"THE CONFUSION OF TONGUES"

This cartoon, which appeared six months after the end of the Abyssinian war, reflects on the aftermath.

The nations had been erecting sanctions as a Tower of Babel (Gen. 11, 1–9). When the whole venture failed, they fell into confused recriminations – 'Babel' is a play on the word for 'confusion' – and argue in their separate languages, without comprehension. 'World peace' cries to Heaven in despair.

Sanctions against Italy were eventually abandoned, but the legacy of recriminatory hostility – not merely between the League powers on one side and Italy on the other, but also among the League powers themselves – remained behind.

15

The Rhineland, 1936

Even before the Abyssinian affair was over, Germany struck another blow at the structure established at Versailles. It will be recalled that the Rhineland had been occupied by the French and Belgians. At the Locarno Conference of 1925, Germany had agreed that, when the Allies withdrew, they would not enter the Rhineland themselves. This was linked to the Franco–Polish and Franco–Czech treaties. The idea was that if France was ever required to vindicate those treaties, she would have easy access to her eastern Allies. In 1930, the French and Belgians withdrew from the Rhineland, which was thenceforth completely demilitarized.

Early in 1936, the Franco–Soviet discussions, which had lain dormant for several months, were revived, and soon the Mutual Assistance Treaty was almost ready for formal ratification. The Germans protested bitterly, claiming that vindication of the treaty by France would involve use of the demilitarized Rhineland in a manner never contemplated at Locarno. If France was in breach of Locarno, the German argument ran, then the arrangements were no longer binding on Germany. And so, on 7 March 1936, German troops entered the Rhineland.

The Germans on one side, the French and Russians on the other, made furious accusations of bad faith against each other. The British reaction also calls for comment. The government deplored the German action, although it was powerless to reverse it. There was, however, a very substantial amount of public feeling sometimes expressed in the question, 'Why shouldn't Jerry walk into his own back garden?' It is important to remember that people who thought like that were by no means all Fascists or semi-Fascists. At the time of Versailles in 1919, the most trenchant British critics of the Treaty had been on the political 'left'. Many British people had not forgotten the resentment they felt at the French occupation of the Ruhr in 1923, or at the French pressure exerted against the German–Austrian *Zollverein* in 1931. Such people were often quite pleased to see the balance between France and Germany shifting the other way.

Whether France could have driven out the Germans by force – and, if so, how various other countries would have reacted – has been debated ever since; but she accepted the enormous rebuff. Later, the Franco–Soviet Agreement was ratified, an event which did not give either country much security but generated considerable suspicion against France.

The Rhineland episode was a tremendously serious warning for the future. It demonstrated the fragile character of international treaties, and the unreliability of the arrangements reached at Locarno a decade earlier.

Cartoon 15.1 Ring-around-the-Nazi! *Los Angeles Times,* 2 March 1936

This American cartoon of early March 1936 comments approvingly on the arrangements for a Franco–Soviet Mutual Assistance Pact, which had reached an advanced stage by this date, but had not yet been ratified. The arrangements were seen as an effective way of 'encircling' Germany, and preventing military expansion in either direction.

Although this cartoon appeared in a Californian newspaper, very remote indeed from Europe, and although Hitler's Germany had not at that date committed external aggression, yet the curved surface – evidently meant to represent the whole earth – on which the three figures stand suggests that the artist perceived the Nazis as a world, and not merely a European, threat.

Cartoon 15.2 The march of events. *Daily Express*, London, 9 March 1936

THE MARCH OF EVENTS

This cartoon appeared two days after the German reoccupation of the Rhineland.

The diplomats have come to the conclusion that the League of Nations would 'never allow' the reoccupation to take place, and that the Locarno arrangements forbade it. The Nazis have ignored such considerations, and proceeded with the occupation.

One of the many marks of developing international anarchy during the later 1930s was the devaluation not only of the League of Nations as an international organization, but also of international treaties.

Cartoon 15.3 'Mirnoe' rychanie fashisma. *Izvestiya*, Moscow, 10 March 1936

„МИРНОЕ" РЫЧАНИЕ ФАШИЗМА

Примечание Бор. Ефимова
«мир» (mir) — по-немецки означает «мне».

'The peaceful snarl of Fascism' is a Soviet comment on the German reoccupation of the Rhineland.

The Nazi militarist has Hitler's familiar hair-style, but the face of a pig. He grasps towards the Rhineland, and probably much more besides, uttering 'Mir!'. As the text points out, this word (which in Russian means 'peace', although it can have other meanings as well in that language) means in German 'to me'.

The representation of the 'Fascist' as a pig, and his association with a skull-and-crossbones and a vulture, is more direct than anything which cartoonists in European countries, or the United States, would have been likely to use at that date.

In the 'Fascist's' left hand, a document marked 'Locarno' is being shredded.

Cartoon 15.4 Rhein-Pakt. *Völkischer Beobachter*, Munich, 14 March 1936

„ . . . tut mir leid, Madame, aber ihr Chauffeur hat mich schon vor einer Woche überfahren und einfach liegenlassen!"

This cartoon appeared in the Nazi *Völkischer Beobachter* just after the German reoccupation of the Rhineland. Marianne appeals to the 'Rhine Pact' – the Locarno agreement over the Rhineland. The Pact lies shattered and helpless in the road and explains to Marianne that a week ago 'her chauffeur' – the Soviet Union – ran him over.

The argument is that Marianne could no longer count on the 'Rhine Pact' because the new Mutual Assistance Treaty with the Soviet Union had destroyed its value.

Cartoon 15.5 Der russische Hypnotiseur. *Simplicissimus*, Munich, 15 March 1936

„Geh nur, Mütterchen, geh nur . . .!"

This is another expression of the German view about the Franco-Soviet Mutual Assistance Pact. As the hypnotized Marianne walks towards the cliff edge, her Russian hypnotist urges her forward.

France is seen not so much as an enemy but as a victim. The contrast between German cartoons of this period and those of a few years earlier, where France is seen as a hostile power armed to the teeth, is considerable.

Cartoon 15.6 Patriotes. *Marianne*, Paris, 18 March 1936

PATRIOTES
— Quelle catastrophe!
— Oui. Hitler a dénoncé le traité...
— Mais non. le Sénat a ratifié le pacte franco-soviétique!...

While some French people welcomed the Franco–Soviet Mutual Assistance Pact, others reacted in a manner not very different from that suggested in the preceding German cartoon (Cartoon 15.5), regarding it as an unmitigated disaster for their country.

This French cartoon appeared shortly after the German reoccupation of the Rhineland. Two French 'patriots' meet in the street. One deplores the 'catastrophe' which has just taken place. The second man imagines that he is referring to Hitler's denunciation of Locarno and occupation of the Rhineland. The first corrects him, and explains that the 'catastrophe' was the Senate's ratification of the Franco–Soviet Pact.

In the next few years, many Frenchmen felt so bitter about any kind of alliance with the Soviet Union that they were prepared to tolerate an accommodation with Germany.

'Belgium withdraws into private life' is a German comment on King Leopold III's declaration of Belgian neutrality and repudiation of the former alliance with France, issued in October 1936. The Belgian government was deeply concerned about the Franco–Soviet Pact, and the German reoccupation of the Rhineland. They had lost the protection of a demilitarized Rhineland, without acquiring – as France had done – the real or imaginary protection of the Soviet treaty.

The Belgian sits quietly in his room, and refuses Marianne's blandishments in favour of a more active life. The poem at the bottom, described as a free translation of the Latin 'Beatus ille homo' – 'Blessed is that man' – reflects on the merits of a quiet existence.

254

Cartoon 15.7 Belgien zieht sich .... *Simplicissimus*,
Munich, 8 November 1936

16

Spain and the triumph of ideology, 1936–9

As cartoons in this book have shown, many people began to notice similarities between Hitler's Nazis and Mussolini's Fascists at least as far back as 1923. Yet nobody took it for granted that this real or apparent ideological similarity implied that countries ruled by those political systems would necessarily become allies if any great conflict were to arise in the future. Right down to the time of Stresa in 1935, it seemed much more likely that they would be enemies. In the same way, France and Britain had political similarities, for both were parliamentary democracies; but at certain times many people in each of those countries regarded the other more as an enemy than as a friend. There was nothing strange or unfamiliar about that sort of thing. From the 1890s until 1917, the French Republic and the Russian Empire, whose political systems were about as different as those of any two countries then existing in Europe, nevertheless functioned as diplomatic, and eventually as military, allies.

In the middle 1930s, international patterns began to become much more closely linked with real or imagined similarities of ideology. Some developments in that direction could be discerned in the latter part of 1935 and the early part of 1936. The Abyssinian question bitterly divided Britain and France on one side from Italy on the other, and thereafter it was almost inevitable that Italy should be drawn to the only other available 'pole of attraction', which was Germany. The Rhineland crisis of March 1936, which might have been expected to restore the 'Stresa Front', failed to do so because the Abyssinian issue was too deep.

By this period, the Soviet Union was playing a much more active part in European politics than she had done for many years. As we have seen, the old Soviet view had been that the real issue of world politics lay between the USSR on one side and all the 'capitalist' states on the other; but a growing appreciation of the direct military threat posed by Nazi Germany made this view give way to a new policy of encouraging alliances designed to contain Germany, and possibly Japan. This new policy first led the Soviet Union to join the League of Nations, and later led to the Mutual Defence Treaty of 1936 with France, which provided the excuse for German reoccupation of the Rhineland. Later in the same year came an important treaty between the Soviet Union and Czechoslovakia, which will later demand closer study.

These moves towards military alliances were associated with a pattern of more strictly 'ideological' behaviour, which also received strong encouragement from the Soviet Union. The various Communist Parties began to argue strongly for the establishment of 'Popular Fronts' in other countries, and particularly the parliamentary democracies. These 'Popular Fronts' were designed to embrace almost every shade of opinion from Communism, through various shades of Socialism and Liberalism, to the milder forms of Conservatism. The 'Popular Fronts' were to be alliances in favour of immediate measures of social and economic reform which were more or less acceptable to all of the disparate parties. The 'Popular Fronts' would also strongly oppose any disruption of the international status quo by 'Fascist' governments.

The 'Popular Front' idea was received in different ways in different countries. In Britain, where there was a strong tradition of one-party governments, the Labour Party had a fair hope of becoming the government without assistance from anybody else in the foreseeable future, and was not disposed to form a 'Popular Front' with anybody else; it saw the minuscule Communist Party in particular as much more of an embarrassment than an asset. In France, where most governments had been coalitions for a very long time and the Communists were far stronger, the 'Popular Front' idea was much more successful. The first actual victory of a 'Popular Front' was at the Spanish general election of February 1936, and this was followed by a similar victory in France a few months later.

The victory of the 'Popular Front' in Spain was followed in July by a military rising, which soon came to be headed by General Francisco Franco. Thus began the Spanish Civil War, which attracted immense attention throughout the world, and continued until Franco's eventual victory early in 1939.

Within a short time of the outbreak of the Civil War, the insurgents were receiving massive assistance from Italy and Germany, while the government was receiving similar assistance from the Soviet Union. An 'International Brigade' of volunteers from many countries fought on the government side. Whether the Brigade exerted much influence on the course of events is doubtful; but its activities – indeed, its very existence – exerted a great influence on the thought of many people, particularly young people, who came to see the struggle in Spain as a matter of universal and not merely Spanish significance.

The British and French governments did what they could to promote the idea of 'non-intervention' by other powers in Spain. The principle was generally acknowledged; its application was widely ignored. Within a short time it became clear that, if either side lost its external support, the other would soon win the war.

The Spanish Civil War was fought with exceptional savagery by both sides, and often the brutalities had little relation to any perceived military advantage which they might confer. Neither side was in any sense monolithic, and each contained people with very different ideas. On the government side, in particular, the various factions often acted in a manner designed not to defeat the common enemy but to secure some local advantage against others fighting ostensibly on the same 'side'.

The importance of the Spanish Civil War lies not so much in what happened but in what people thought was happening. Franco's cause brought together the Italian and German governments as fighting allies in a common cause. On the other side, an extremely wide range of opinion sympathized with the government. In Britain, for example, the Labour, Liberal and Communist Parties were more or less unanimous in giving eager support to the Spanish government. Considerable numbers of Conservatives did the same, and only a small minority positively favoured Franco's cause.

The more or less official attitude of the National Government in Britain was that it did not care much which side won, provided that it was a 'Spanish' victory; what it feared was that a victory for Franco would become in effect a victory for the 'Fascist' governments of Italy and Germany. The French 'Popular Front' Government felt natural political sympathy with its Spanish counterpart; but it was dissuaded, partly by British influence, from giving more positive support. Among the major powers, only the Soviet government gave unambigiuous support to the Spanish government.

Thus a real polarization of opinion was brought about. The 'Fascist' powers were brought together, despite their real and continuing differences of interest, while, on the other side, a sort of ideological 'Popular Front' came into existence – a very widespread frame of mind which did not enquire too closely about the differences of objectives and practice between the various parties of the 'left' and 'centre', including the Communists.

Once matters had settled into this kind of simplistic dichotomy, the chances of international peace being long preserved became remote. International disputes were no longer regarded as complex quarrels over interests, which might be resolved by a common interest in preserving peace, but rather as disputes over fundamental ideology, in which no quarter was possible.

Cartoon 16.1 A la bataille de Poitiers. *Marianne*, Paris, 2 September 1936

A LA BATAILLE DE POITIERS
Les Maures : — C'est malin de nous repousser ! Vous aurez peut-être besoin de nous un jour pour vous débarrasser du Front populaire !

The Spanish Civil War began with a military insurrection in Spanish Morocco, and, in the early part of the fighting in Spain itself, Moorish troops who were of Moslem faith played a substantial part on Franco's side. This did not strengthen the claim made by some of his supporters that he was acting as a 'patriot' and in defence of 'Christian' values.

This cartoon appeared in the French periodical *Marianne*, whose politics might be described as 'left of centre'. It alludes to an incident in French history which would have been familiar to its readers. In the early eighth century, the Moors, invading from north Africa, brought Spain under Moslem domination, and then invaded France. They were defeated by the Franks under Charles Martel, grandfather of Charlemagne, at the battle of Poitiers in 732. Historians debate the importance or otherwise of that battle; but by some people it has been regarded as one of the 'decisive battles of history', which prevented the Moslems dominating France and perhaps even Britain.

In this cartoon, the battle of Poitiers is given a topical twist. The retreating Moors cry to the victorious Franks, 'It's wrong to push us back! Perhaps you will need us one day to get rid of the Popular Front.' The implication is that the Moors, who were currently fighting against the 'Popular Front' Government in Spain, might also be used against the new 'Popular Front' Government in France.

259

Cartoon 16.2 The autograph collector. *Evening Standard*, London, 8 January 1937

THE AUTOGRAPH COLLECTOR   (Copyright in All Countries.)

Soon after the failure of the 'Hoare–Laval Pact' over Abyssinia at the end of 1936, Anthony Eden became British Foreign Secretary. In this cartoon of early 1937, Eden seeks the 'autographs' of Hitler and Mussolini, both of whom were actively helping Franco, in support of the British government's proposals for 'non-intervention' in Spain. The cartoonist implies that his efforts will prove unsuccessful – indeed, even if they succeeded they would not halt the march of Fascism.

It is striking to note that by this date Hitler and Mussolini were already presented as close allies – a remarkable contrast with the state of affairs a couple of years earlier.

At the time when this cartoon was drawn, there was a considerable public 'craze' for seeking the autographs of celebrities.

Cartoon 16.3 Ocherednoy 'otvet'. *Pravda*, Moscow, 11 January 1937

OЧЕРЕДНОЙ «ОТВЕТ».   Рисунок худ. Кукрыниксы.

This Soviet cartoon, 'Reply in turn', which appeared a few days after Cartoon 16.2, is more bitter. Mussolini, driving the 'voluntary tank' with the flying pennant 'To Spain', spits out contemptuously his 'Note', which is received obsequiously, though regretfully, by the waiting British or French diplomat.

In theory, Italian and German forces assisting Franco were 'volunteers' – hence the name on the tank. In early January 1937, several diplomatic 'Notes' relating to aspects of the war in Spain were exchanged between Britain and France on one side and Germany and Italy on the other. The ones to which the cartoon alludes were concerned with checking the use of non-Spanish 'volunteers' in Spain.

Cartoon 16.4 Die internationale Brigade. *Simplicissimus,* Munich, 31 January 1937

This German cartoon concerns another group of foreign volunteers in Spain: the 'International Brigade' which was fighting on the side of the Spanish government. One International Brigade soldier complains that 'I'm thoroughly confused. Are we Anarchists, Communists, Bolsheviks or members of the "Red Guard"?'. The reply is that 'We are all Spaniards. Valencia [seat of the Spanish government at the time] has naturalized us.'

Two points are made here. First, there is a sort of riposte to the common criticism of Franco that he was relying on foreign help. So, too, was the Spanish government, although it had gone through the formality of giving its foreign supporters Spanish nationality. The second point is that the International Brigade (and, indeed, the Spanish government itself) was of very mixed political complexion, and those who were fighting in its support for ideological reasons could not be by any means sure that it was their own ideology which would win if the Spanish government was successful.

Cartoon 16.5 Qu'on se le dise. *Le Canard Enchaîné*, Paris, 31 March 1937

QU'ON SE LE DISE

— *D'abord, le Duce n a pas de troupes en Espagne, et ensuite, il ne les rappellera pas !*

This French cartoon also comments on 'non-intervention' in Spain. Two men – one of them evidently a wealthy sympathizer with Franco – are in conversation. One says to the other, 'First, the Duce hasn't got any troops in Spain, and second, he isn't going to withdraw them!'

Technically, Italians fighting in Spain were 'volunteers', and the Italian government was not formally involved. It is probably fair to say that enthusiastic supporters for both sides in the Spanish Civil War were not very concerned about the objective truth or falsehood of criticisms made by their opponents, or whether the arguments advanced against them were logical and consistent.

While the 'left' in both Britain and France was almost unanimously pro-Spanish government, there were perceptible differences between attitudes of the 'right' in the two countries. In Britain, the 'right of centre' National Government, and most of its supporters, were primarily concerned to ensure that the issue, however decided, should be settled by Spaniards and not by foreigners. In France, many people on the 'right' were strongly in support of Franco, and cared little whether he was supported by non-Spanish forces or not.

Cartoon 16.6 Prozhorlivy izhdivenetz. *Izvestiya*, Moscow, 20 September 1938

ПРОЖОРЛИВЫЙ ИЖДИВЕНЕЦ

Рис. Бор. Ефимова.

— Ч-чорт!.. Его аппетит растет обратно пропорционально его успехам...

This Soviet cartoon, 'Greedy dependant', concerns Fascist intervention in Spain. Hitler and Mussolini shovel great numbers of men and weapons out of boxes labelled 'From Italy' and 'From Germany' into the mouth of Franco. Mussolini, pausing from his exertions, says, 'Devil! His appetite grows in inverse proportion to his success . . .'

The implication is that German and Italian commitment to Franco was hardly worthwhile; for in this period of the war it was costing them dearly, but producing little positive effect.

ARENE OU ABATTOIR?

La mise à mort du taureau.

(*Bru, Opera Mundi*)

266

Cartoon 16.7 Arène ou abbatoir? *Marianne*, Paris, 10 August 1938

'Arena or abbatoir?' asks this French cartoon, drawn at a time when the Spanish Civil War was far from finished, but its issue was hardly in doubt.

Surrounding Spain are various flags, including the Union Jack on Gibraltar and the Italian flag flying on the Balearic Islands (which were temporarily in Italian occupation).

In the 'killing of the bull', the suffering Spanish bull is impaled by various weapons, including three which bear insignia of the Soviet Union, Germany and Italy respectively. There is also a crescent and five-pointed Islamic star, alluding to the many Moslems fighting in Spain.

Cartoon 16.8 Shades of success. *Punch*, London, 1 February 1939

SHADES OF SUCCESS

This British cartoon was drawn early in 1939, at a time when it was clear that Franco was going to win. The General surveys a map of Spain, while the 'shades' of Hitler and Mussolini look on. The implication is that Franco's victory would have been impossible without help from the other two dictators.

The political views of *Punch* in this period were by no means 'left-wing'; but the attitude suggested is very different from that of the Frenchman in Cartoon 16.5. In Britain, Hitler and Mussolini were by this date coming to be seen more and more as likely enemies in the foreseeable future. The overwhelming majority of British people of all political persuasions regarded Franco's impending victory as regrettable.

Cartoon 16.9 'Vous me raconterez . . .' *Le Canard Enchaîné*, Paris, 8 March 1939

— Vous me raconterez votre défense de Verdun en 16 et je vous raconterai mes prises de Madrid en 36, 37, 38 et 39.

At the end of February 1939, when there was no remaining doubt about the outcome of the Spanish Civil War, Britain and France formally transferred diplomatic recognition from the former Spanish government to General Franco's regime. The first French ambassador appointed was Marshal Pétain, who had acquired an enormous reputation as a wise and humane military commander in the First World War, but who was to head the 'Vichy Government' in France less than sixteen months after this cartoon was drawn.

In this cartoon, Franco and Pétain meet, with a Moorish soldier standing guard. Franco says to Pétain, 'You tell me about your defence of Verdun in '16, and I shall tell you about my captures of Madrid in '36, '37, '38 and '39.' This alludes to the very protracted and 'ding-dong' character of the Spanish Civil War, in which for a very long time each side made considerable military advances and seemed poised for final victory. In fact, Madrid did not fall until almost the end of the Civil War, although on several occasions it was seriously threatened.

Both Pétain and Franco were very familiar figures to Frenchmen of the time, and there was no need for the cartoonist to identify either man for the benefit of his readers.

17

Problems of foreign policy,
1936–8

In the middle and late 1930s, all major countries were compelled to review their foreign policies. We have already noted some features of this general review. The Soviet Union had decided that the great threat came from Nazi Germany, and was actively encouraging alliances designed to frustrate that threat. Italian policy was becoming increasingly aggressive, while Germany and Italy were drawing together, despite continuing differences of interest in central Europe.

Japan was also drawn increasingly towards alliance with Germany – neither country being inhibited by the Nazi doctrines of 'Aryan race-superiority'. The 'Anti-Comintern Pact' between the two countries was set up in November 1936, and a year later it was broadened to include Italy. In theory, the Anti-Comintern Pact was a device for containing the 'world revolution' aspirations of the Communist International; in practice it became more a device for cooperation in policies of international aggression, whether these related to the Soviet Union or not. Thus in the second half of 1937 Japan became involved in large-scale fighting against China, while Germany looked on benevolently. The serious prospect began to emerge that Germany, Italy and Japan would link together in a good deal more aggression against many other victims.

How should Britain and France respond to all this? Superficially, they seemed enormously strong. The British navy and the French army were widely regarded as equal, or superior, to any corresponding force in the world. Traditionally, the two countries had relied on their own weapons, and to some extent on international alliances, for defence of their possessions and interests, and on the League of Nations for preservation of international stability.

In the 1930s, the efficacy of all these devices was being called into question. After Manchuria, and particularly after Abyssinia, it was impossible to see the League of Nations as an effective defence against the aggression of any great power. France was increasingly apprehensive that her army was being overshadowed by that of Germany, while both Britain and France were uneasily conscious of the growing importance of air power. Britain was to some extent reacting by building a substantial air force; but the French air force remained rudimentary. France, however, was establishing a powerful line of military fortifications – the Maginot

Line – along her frontier with Germany; but her other eastern frontiers were relatively unprotected.

The system of international alliances was breaking down. France's mutual assistance pacts with Czechoslovakia and Poland began to look like dangerous commitments which would operate to her disadvantage. Indeed, the position of Poland in relation to France had been in considerable doubt since the German–Polish Non-aggression Pact 1934. As for the Franco–Soviet Mutual Assistant Pact which was completed in 1936, this was a source of both political and military embarrassment, as well as possible benefit.

And finally there was the extremely gloomy prospect which Service advisers held before Britain and France. Whether or not they could contain one of the three potential aggressors, Germany, Italy and Japan, there was little doubt that a war against all three, with no substantial ally, would result in defeat.

Would a substantial ally appear if the test came? There were two countries which might tip the scale. The Soviet Union was an obvious candidate. But how effective would the Soviet Union prove as an ally? This question became increasingly poignant in the late 1930s, as Stalin's infamous purges were extended from civilian victims to the Red Army. Perhaps two-thirds of the Soviet High Command 'disappeared'; and it was difficult to believe that such an army would prove of much military value for a long time, save perhaps in defence of its own territory.

The other possible ally was the United States. Anyone glancing through American sources of the time is left without a shadow of doubt about two matters. The first was very encouraging. Practically all Americans deplored the aggression that Italy and Japan had already committed, and were deeply apprehensive that Germany would engage in future adventures. The second was much less encouraging; for the overwhelming majority of Americans were determined to keep the United States out of any future war which might occur.

Thus in the late 1930s Britain and France were faced with an exceedingly difficult and rapidly deteriorating international situation, and there was no quarter to which they could confidently look for help on the scale required. In the earlier part of the decade, they had more or less reacted to individual situations as they arose, with little sign of any long-term policy. This was no longer an adequate policy.

The first initiative for a new approach came from Britain. In May 1937, Neville Chamberlain succeeded Stanley Baldwin as Prime Minister. The policy always associated with the name of Chamberlain is called 'appeasement'. That word has acquired so many pejorative overtones that it is important to recall what it meant at the time.

It required no genius to see that many important international changes would occur in the next few years, whatever Britain might do. In Chamberlain's view, it was possible to engineer international agreements effecting those changes which – while no doubt unsatisfactory in many respects – would nevertheless be kept, and would be infinitely preferable to war.

That view was by no means universally held in Britain. As often happens when new issues arise, attitudes did not follow closely the lines of political parties. Critics of the appeasement policy, of whom by far the most important was Winston Churchill, began to appear in the ranks of Conservatives and other supporters of the National Government. Those critics were disposed to argue instead for a policy of 'collective security': that Britain should seek to organize countries which seemed to be under threat in a common resistance against aggression. The opposition parties – Labour and the Liberals – also seemed to favour collective security, although there remained considerable elements in both parties whose approach was more in tune with the popular pacifism of ten years earlier; and many members of the Labour Party never found it possible to swallow the idea that massive rearmament was necessary if collective security was to become effective.

Cartoon 17.1 'How happily . . . ' *Evening Standard*, London, 22 May 1936

This cartoon (see p. 274) appeared in May 1936, shortly after the end of the Italo–Abyssinian war, and before renewed difficulties with Japan arose. Foreign Secretary Anthony Eden, as the policeman, deliberates how to deal with the dangers of both Hitler and Mussolini, in a parody of the famous Gilbert and Sullivan song.

Mussolini is laden with 'swag'. The problem with Hitler concerned the future rather than the present. Thus far, Nazi Germany had not transgressed international frontiers,* but there was good reason for thinking that she had ambitions on a huge scale. Hitler's book, *Mein Kampf*, left no doubt about the Führer's own ideas on the matter, while both the German rearmament decision of 1935 and the occupation of the Rhineland a year later were widely seen as steps in that direction.

Thus far, Hitler and Mussolini were not closely associated. But how could Britain, even with cooperation from France, deal successfully with both dictators?

---

* Acquisition of the Saar in 1935 had followed a properly organized plebiscite, clearly represented the wishes of the great majority of people in the area concerned, and was freely acknowledged by all the powers.

"HOW HAPPILY COULD I DEAL WITH EITHER, WERE T'OTHER DEAR CHARMER AWAY."

274

Cartoon 17.2 Stocks still. *Daily Mail*, London, 7 November 1936

STOCKS STILL—*By POY*

Mr. Eden, in his statement on Foreign Policy, rightly stressed the need of rearmament, but still insisted on continued adherence to the League of Nations.

Some elements of the British press which gave general support to the National Government were nevertheless critical of its continued support for the League of Nations, for this carried the implication that Britain might become involved in disputes where her own interests were not directly affected – as had already happened over Abyssinia.

This *Daily Mail* cartoon expresses that point of view. John Bull is strengthening his arms (a pun) by rearmament; but his legs are still imprisoned in the stocks 'Geneva' – i.e. the League of Nations – where they are firmly padlocked by Eden's foreign policy.

Cartoon 17.3 Komintern am Werk. *Simplicissimus*, Munich, 13 December 1936

Komintern am Werk

(Karl Arnold)

In Spanien

„Hier herrscht in der Tat ewiger Friede! Wir wollen den Ossietzky nicht unterschätzen, aber den Friedens-Nobelpreis hätten eigentlich wir bekommen müssen."

In Frankreich

„Allons, Marianne, unsere Sowjets wollen endlich Taten sehen!"

Das Ziel

„Es ist absolut gleichgültig, ob 90 v. H. der Menschen zugrunde gehen, wenn nur die restlichen 10 v. H. zuverlässige Kommunisten sind, die die Existenz der Sowjets sicherstellen . . ."   Lenin

Deutsch-japanische Abwehrfront
„HALT!!"

276

This German cartoon of December 1936 – 'Comintern at work' – comments on the German–Japanese 'Anti-Comintern Pact' which had come into existence in the previous month. Italy was still not a member at this stage.

In the first quadrant, 'In Spain', the Comintern agent, standing with international spectators amid the desolation produced by the Civil War, rejoices that 'Here eternal peace really rules!' and claims entitlement to the Nobel Peace Prize for the Comintern's efforts. In the second quadrant, 'In France', the Comintern agent, who has deluded Marianne into concluding the Franco–Soviet Pact, incites her to plant a bomb, telling her that 'our Soviets want to see some action'.

The third quadrant, 'The target', shows Death carrying the hammer and sickle, and quotes from Lenin: 'It is a matter of absolute indifference if 90 per cent of the human race perish, provided that the remaining 10 per cent are reliable Communists, who will secure the existence of the Soviets.'

In the final quadrant, the 'German–Japanese Defence Front', in the character of an armed angel equipped also with a pen, declares 'Halt!!' to the advancing figure of Litvinov, Soviet Commissar for Foreign Affairs.

Cartoon 17.4 Tour d'horizon. *Le Canard Enchaîné*, Paris, 20 January 1937

TOUR D'HORIZON

— Rome ! La ville aux sept collines... De gauche à droite, le Tyrol, les Karpathes, les Balkans, le massif éthiopien, le Rif, la sierra Guadarama, et les Alpes de Savoie...

This French cartoon of January 1937 comments both on Mussolini's wide ambitions and on the increasingly cordial relations which were developing between Italy and Germany.

Mussolini is entertaining the German Air Force chief, General Goering. The Duce eulogizes the scene, and the area of current, or intended, Italian influence: 'Rome! The city of seven hills . . . . From left to right, the Tyrol, the Carpathians, the Balkans, the Ethiopian massif, the [North African] Rif, the Guadarama sierra, and the Savoy Alps . . .'

Nazi cartoons about the Soviet Union seem to alternate between those – like Cartoon 17.3 – which suggest that Communism is an extremely dangerous enemy and those like Cartoon 17.5 which suggest that it has reduced Russia to a condition of extreme weakness.

'The enemy within' alludes to the 'purges' which Stalin was operating in the USSR against people who were accused of being 'Trotskyites' – that is, followers of the disgraced and exiled former Bolshevik leader Leon Trotsky. Stalin, as the physician, addresses the ailing woman: 'It is only the Trotsky germs which are making you ill, Little Mother Russia! There-

Cartoon 17.5 Der innere Feind. *Simplicissimus*, Munich, 18 April 1937

Der innere Feind

(Erich Schilling)

„Es sind nur die Trotzki-Bazillen, die dich krank machen, Mütterchen Rußland! Darum mußt du recht fleißig meine Medizin nehmen." — „Ach, Väterchen Stalin, ich weiß nicht, woran ich schneller sterben werde, an den Bazillen oder an deiner Medizin!"

fore you must diligently take my medicine.' Russia replies, 'Ah, Little Father Stalin, I don't know whether I shall die more quickly from the germs or from your medicine!'

Certainly Stalin's 'purges' were causing immense suffering in the Soviet Union, were deeply alienating many people in the country to the regime, and were gravely weakening the Red Army. This process was making the country far more vulnerable to the hostile ambitions of Nazi Germany.

Cartoon 17.6 Good luck to both! *News of the World,* London, 30 May 1937

GOOD LUCK TO BOTH!

This cartoon commemorates the retirement of Prime Minister Stanley Baldwin and the succession of Neville Chamberlain on 28 May 1937. The new captain of the 'Ship of State' and the old salute each other in a friendly and respectful fashion, and there is nothing to suggest that the new man will pilot the vessel in a different direction from his predecessor.

Baldwin and Chamberlain had both long held high public office, and were both Conservatives. In Baldwin's third and last ministry (1935–7), however, he had shown some lassitude. Chamberlain, already in his late sixties, was only a couple of years younger than Baldwin, but he showed considerably more vigour. He had a much clearer idea of the direction of foreign policy which he sought to follow, and this policy of 'appeasement' was to prove of enormous importance in the next two years.

Cartoon 17.7 The Trojan horse. *Daily Express*, London, 29 January 1937

THE TROJAN HORSE

CRIPPS: "Very well, if you won't have it inside I'll take it on tour, and let everybody see what a good thing you've missed."

These two cartoons reflect, from different political angles, on the problems facing British opposition parties in relation to foreign policy questions of the later 1930s.

The first cartoon, 'The Trojan horse', deals with the campaign in favour of a 'Popular Front' composed of all critics of the British government, rather like the 'Popular Fronts' which had already formed the governments in France and Spain. A 'Popular Front' would be concerned with domestic as well as international issues; but in the circumstances of the time foreign policy would certainly loom very large in its programme.

The 'Popular Front' idea was welcomed by the Communist Party, by the Independent Labour Party (ILP) which had broken from the Labour Party in 1932, and (to some extent) by the Liberal Party. The Labour Party (commonly called the 'Socialist Party' by its critics) was much more sceptical, although some Labour Party members, notably Sir Stafford Cripps, campaigned eagerly in support.

Cartoon 17.8 'To make you fit!' *Daily Herald*, London, 9 February 1937

"To Make You Fit!"—"*Yes, but Fit for What!*"

In Cartoon 17.7, the 'Popular Front' (or 'United Front') idea is regarded by the Labour Party within the fortress as a 'Trojan horse' on Communist wheels and ILP legs. Herbert Morrison, Clement Attlee and Ernest Bevin are seen among the battlements. Cripps proposes to 'take it on tour' – in other words, to campaign nationally for a 'Popular Front'. Cripps was expelled from the Labour Party for his pains, although he was later received back, and became an important minister in the 1945 Labour Government.

The second cartoon, from the Labour *Daily Herald*, refers to the children's story of the 'Three Little Pigs'. The 'big, bad wolf', 'War needs', offers the inducement of '£2,000,000 physical jerks' – a government-sponsored physical fitness campaign – to the feeble-looking piglets, with the evident intention of fattening them for his own requirements.

This cartoon is very much in the pacifist vein which characterized Labour cartoons of the 1920s and early 1930s. It fitted in less convincingly, however, with the current foreign policy ideas of the Labour Party, which was becoming more and more insistent that aggression should be met by 'firm' policies. The Labour Party – and, indeed, the opposition in general – had considerable difficulty in the late 1930s in reconciling its earlier views with the new problems posed by the rise of 'Fascism'.

Cartoon 17.9 Dieu: 'Tu gagneras ton pain . . .' *Marianne,*
Paris, 13 April 1938

These two cartoons of 1938 cast light on some of France's problems.

The first reflects on the country's economy. While most of Europe had largely recovered economically from the Depression by the later 1930s, France (which had suffered little in the earlier part of the decade) was experiencing heavy unemployment.

God addresses the unemployed man with the curse of Adam: 'In the sweat of thy face shalt thou eat bread . . .' (Gen. 3, 19). The unexpected reply is, 'Lord, that's all that I ask.'

Cartoon 17.10 Par ces temps ... *Marianne*, Paris, 23 March 1938

PAR CES TEMPS DE MAUVAISE GRIPPE

Marianne. – 'Heureusement que j'ai une bonne couverture! . . .'

The second cartoon considers France's garments 'for these times of bad influenza'. Marianne, equipped with the warm wrap 'Maginot Line', faces icy blasts from Hitler and Mussolini with the reflection: 'Fortunately I have a good cloak.'

The 'Line', however, was a purely defensive work. France's foreign policy required her to be able to issue a realistic threat of action beyond her own frontiers in support of other countries. A country with such powerful fortifications was unlikely to venture outside them.

Cartoon 17.11 Look out for a tail-spin! *New York Times,* 18 July 1937

Look out for a tail-spin!

This American cartoon from July 1937 comments on the renewed Japanese aggression against China. Japan, who has already cut off Manchuria from the tail of the Chinese dragon, prepares to cut off another segment from the beast, who turns round in anger.

The Chinese cause attracted strong sympathy in the United States on idealistic, but also on economic, grounds; for the Americans were disturbed at the prospect that they would be excluded from Chinese markets if Japan came to control them.

Perhaps there is some wishful thinking in the cartoon; for a 'dragon' which had already allowed part of its tail to be amputated is not likely to prove very effective in defending the remainder.

In this period, and for years afterwards, there was some doubt among American policy-formers as to whether – if they must choose – eastern Asia or Europe was of more importance.

Cartoon 17.12 Les Japonais à Pékin. *Le Canard Enchaîné,* Paris, 22 December 1937

LES JAPONAIS A PÉKIN

— Un coup pour la bonne, Excellence, et deux coups pour le nouveau gouvernement chinois.

The renewed Japanese attack on China in 1937 was marked by some features which would later be emulated elsewhere. War was not formally declared by Japan but, at the turn of 1937–8, the Japanese broke off diplomatic relations with the regular Chinese government and established a 'satellite' Chinese regime which they were able to dominate.

This French cartoon comments cynically on these events. The Chinese porter shows the Japanese officer to his room, where the portrait of the Chinese leader Chiang Kai-shek has been replaced by that of the Mikado. The porter addresses the officer, 'One ring for the chambermaid, Your Excellency, and two rings for the new Chinese government.' Evidently, both of them could be regarded equally as servants at the disposal of the Japanese.

Cartoon 17.13 Some day the worm will turn. *Chicago Tribune*, 19 July 1936

Cartoon 17.14 Don't let 'em fool you too, son. *New Leader,* London, 18 September 1938

Don't let 'em fool you too, son

In the late 1930s, most political cartoons in most countries were preoccupied with some sort of perceived 'threat', and implied that the people of their respective countries should be prepared in appropriate circumstances to go to war to counter that 'threat'.

Cartoons 17.13, 17.14 and 17.15 present a different point of view. One is drawn from an American newspaper generally considered to stand on the far 'right', the other two from a British newspaper – the organ of the ILP – considered to stand on the far 'left'.

The *Chicago Tribune* suggests that 'European cannon fodder', whose willingness to fight made previous wars possible, should 'strike' against

Cartoon 17.15 Look! They are your enemies! *New Leader*, London, 18 September 1938

LOOK! They are your ENEMIES!

any future war in which the statesmen might become involved. It reflects on the hypocrisy which often accompanied public statements of the politicians. The *Chicago Tribune* argued strenuously against American participation in wars which were not concerned with America's 'vital interests'; but in this case it also called for 'direct action' by Europeans.

The *New Leader* cartoons make different points. In the first, the soldier of the earlier war rises from his grave to warn his son against the specious appeals which lured him to his own death: appeals on grounds of patriotism ('King and Country'), religion ('Your Church and You'), and even trade unionism ('T.U.C. . . . .'). In the second, a figure with 'Lib[eral], Lab[our], C[ommunist] P[arty]' on his waistcoat attempts to persuade the worker that his 'enemies' are Hitler and Mussolini, while the capitalist picks his pocket – with connivance from the soldier and policeman in the background. This was a traditional socialist argument; but in the circumstances of the time most parties of the 'left' were preoccupied with the foreign threat.

18

Italy, Germany and Austria, 1937–8

The first test for the 'appeasement' policy of Neville Chamberlain arose in connection with Italy. In the spring of 1937, relations between Britain and Italy were poor. Although sanctions over Abyssinia had been abandoned, there was still a considerable legacy from the old policy – which, among other things, made it difficult for Italy to obtain international loans. Italy was responding by stirring up trouble in Arab areas of the Middle East, where Britain was still the paramount power. Neither Britain nor Italy – and certainly not the unfortunate Abyssinians – derived any benefit from the current state of affairs. Although there was cooperation between Italy and Germany in Spain, the two countries were still a long way from resolving their differences in central Europe. Yet, if Britain and Italy did not reach some kind of agreement soon, it was predictable that Mussolini would be driven into the waiting arms of Hitler.

One of Chamberlain's first international initiatives as Prime Minister was to write a personal letter to Mussolini, suggesting that serious efforts be made to resolve their differences. Mussolini replied promptly and eagerly.

Anthony Eden, the Foreign Secretary, had conceived a dislike for Mussolini which at this stage far transcended his dislike for Hitler. He could reasonably have objected to the Prime Minister's action being taken over his head. But he didn't; instead, the Foreign Office used every device of delay.

As the year 1937 wore on, Mussolini seems to have decided that Chamberlain either could not, or would not, deliver the contemplated understanding, and began to look seriously in the only other direction available to him. Soon there were abundant signs of growing warmth between Germany and Italy, and before the year was out Italy had adhered to the 'Anti-Comintern Pact'.

Some time elapsed before the differences between Chamberlain and Eden came to light. Senior members of the Cabinet, and perhaps the Prime Minister himself, did not appreciate how deep they were, or the reason for the delay. The end came with a short, sharp crisis in February 1938, which culminated in Eden's resignation and his replacement by Viscount Halifax.

Chamberlain immediately sought to advance the Italian negotiations;

but before they could progress very far they were overtaken by events. The German government put great pressure on the Austrian Chancellor, Kurt von Schuschnigg, to include some Austrian Nazis in his government. A complex crisis arose, in which events seemed to have advanced faster than, and in different directions from, anybody's original intentions. The upshot was the resignation of Schuschnigg, and soon afterwards German troops moved into Austria. Hitler had certainly long desired *Anschluss* between Germany and Austria, but it seems likely that even he had not intended it to take place at that particular moment and in that particular way. Mussolini made no attempt to intervene; evidently there had been some sort of understanding by which Austria was transferred from the Italian to the German sphere of influence.

In the aftermath, 'plebiscites' were held in both Germany and Austria. Both countries voted, predictably, for *Anschluss*. The majorities in both countries were in excess of 99 per cent, and obviously faked. What the people concerned really thought of the matter remains a point of speculation to this day.

By all tests, the *Anschluss* was an extremely important event. A European frontier had been changed by force, and, if one frontier could be altered in that manner, why not others? As many observers noted, a map of the new 'Greater Germany' looked uncommonly like the head of a wolf, with Czechoslovakia in its maw.

As for the Anglo–Italian negotiations, their most important original purpose – the stabilization of central Europe – had been lost; but they were not entirely pointless, and proceeded to an agreement in a short time. It is arguable that this agreement gave Mussolini some independence of action *vis-à-vis* Hitler, and may perhaps have played some part in keeping Italy out of the eventual war for several months.

Cartoon 18.1 Would you oblige me . . .? *Evening Standard*, 25 February 1938

(Copyright in All Countries.) **WOULD YOU OBLIGE ME WITH A MATCH PLEASE ?**

This is a famous cartoon about Anthony Eden's resignation from the office of Foreign Secretary, in February 1938. Chamberlain, with a portrait of Eden on his lap, foolishly obliges 'Muzzler' – a combination of Hitler and Mussolini – with a match, which Muzzler evidently proposes to deploy in igniting the fuse to the bomb under Chamberlain's seat.

The cartoonist could only go on the evidence available to him, and his interpretation of that evidence was reasonable at the time. But he could not have known (for example) of the earlier correspondence between Chamberlain and Eden which is now available to scholars, and which throws some important light on the story. It now seems clear that Chamberlain was by no means the 'innocent dupe' portrayed in the cartoon. He was well aware of the dangers in the international position, and one of his principal objects in pressing for negotiations with Italy – the main cause of Eden's resignation – was to prevent Mussolini and Hitler being drawn together in an alliance which would shatter the peace of Europe. It is arguable that Eden is much more responsible than Chamberlain for the failure of these efforts.

Cartoon 18.2 Key positions. *Daily Express*, London,
17 February 1938

KEY POSITIONS

This cartoon was drawn even before Eden's resignation, at a time when
pressure was already being exerted by Germany on the Austrian Chancellor Schuschnigg for the inclusion of Nazis in his Cabinet. As it suggests,
the Austrian Nazis were to occupy 'key positions', which would give them
considerable control over the course of events. No doubt their long-term
aim was *Anschluss* – literally, 'connection', but an expression commonly
understood to mean complete union of the two countries. Their immediate
object, however, was probably the introduction of Nazi features into the
Austrian state.

Cartoon 18.3 Rome décadente. *Marianne*, Paris, 23 February 1938

ROME DÉCADENTE

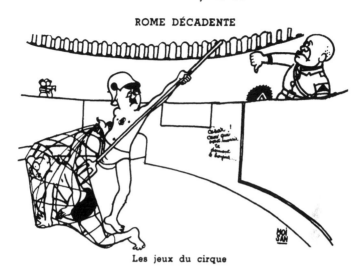

Les jeux du cirque

In this French cartoon, Hitler, as a gladiator in Roman circus-games, has successfully ensnared his rival Schuschnigg. Before delivering the death-blow with his trident, the victorious gladiator must have approval from the Emperor – Mussolini in this cartoon. Mussolini is granting this approval. On the wall is a rough French equivalent of the gladiators' traditional greeting, 'Ave, Caesar; morituri te salutant!' – 'Hail, Caesar; those who are about to die salute you!' The two small figures in the background, who are also giving the 'thumbs down' signal, seem to be wearing German and Italian military uniform.

Even at this date it was clear that Mussolini had given some kind of approval to Hitler, authorizing him to exert pressure on Austria. The relationship between the two dictators was much more equal than it became a year or two later, and many people probably still saw Mussolini as the dominant figure.

Hitler, the poacher, has killed the chamois 'Austrian integrity'. Mussolini, the corrupt gamekeeper, does not propose to interfere with his friend's activities.

The scene is suggestive of the Tyrol. One of the serious differences which had hitherto existed between Italy and Germany concerned the South Tyrol, an area including the town of Brenner, which is largely German-speaking. The South Tyrol had belonged to Austria before the First World War, but was granted to Italy under the peace treaties. Evidently one part of the 'understanding' reached between the two dictators in relation to Austria was an acknowledgement that Germany would not call the Italian position there into question.

Cartoon 18.4 Good hunting. *Punch*, London, 23 February 1938

GOOD HUNTING

MUSSOLINI. "ALL RIGHT, ADOLF—I NEVER HEARD A SHOT."

Cartoon 18.5 La paix allemande. *Marianne*, Paris,
2 March 1938

LA PAIX ALLEMANDE
M. Schuschnigg :
— Jusqu'ici, mais pas plus loin !...

'The German peace' is perhaps a parody of the expression 'Carthaginian peace', meaning total destruction, like that which befell Carthage in 146 BC, at the end of the Third Punic War.

Schuschnigg, who is being swallowed by the serpent which carries the features of Hitler, makes a futile attempt to impose terms: 'Up to here, but no further!'

The dove of peace has dropped its olive branch in fright.

Cartoon 18.6 The juggler. *Washington Post*, 13 March 1938

The Juggler.

This American cartoon appeared just after German troops occupied Austria.

Mussolini, the juggler, has sought to keep several eggs in the air, despite growing difficulties. One of those eggs, 'Austrian independence', has fallen on his head.

While Mussolini acknowledged the *Anschluss* without disapproval, and it was evident that he had in some way authorized it, there could be no doubt that the event was a considerable embarrassment to him.

Carton 18.7 'Os'-to, os' . . .'. *Pravda*, Moscow, 28 March 1938

«Ось-то ось, а рыбку врозь»

Рисунок художников Кукрыниксы.

This Soviet cartoon also notes Mussolini's discomfiture at the *Anschluss*. Hitler and Mussolini are fishing from a jetty. Hitler has hooked the fish 'Austria' and kicks against Mussolini, who is likely to be pushed into the water, in order to gain leverage to land it. Hitler expresses his determination to land the fish, 'Axis or no Axis'.

In this period, the term 'Rome–Berlin Axis' was often used to describe the developing alliance between Hitler and Mussolini.

Cartoon 18.8 Die Erfüllung. *Simplicissimus*, Munich, 3 April 1938

Die Erfüllung

„Auf was mir seit 1918 g'wart' ham — sell iecht mit oam Schlag wahr gword'n."

'The fulfilment' expresses the official German view of the Austrian *Anschluss*. German troops march into an Austrian village, where they are greeted by an enthusiastic welcome and the display of Nazi flags. The Austrian peasant reflects that he has been waiting for this since 1918, and now it has taken place in one blow.

Cartoon 18.9 Anxiété. *Marianne*, Paris, 9 March 1938

ANXIETE

Albion. — Que va-t-il m'arriver si je lui enlève sa camisole ?...

Britannia approaches the bound figure of Mussolini, who is seated on the rickety stool 'Abyssinia'. She asks, 'What will happen to me if I take off his strait-jacket?' The garment carries the words 'Gibraltar' and 'Suez', and Mussolini's expression suggests frustration and anger. Britain's strongly held bases – for example, at Suez and Gibraltar, as indicated in the cartoon – curtailed Italy's designs considerably.

This cartoon is critical of the British government's decision to seek an arrangement with Italy. The implication is that he will, as soon as the opportunity presents itself, attempt mischief of some kind.

Cartoon 18.10 Lord Halifax disposes. *Daily Herald,*
London, 10 May 1938

Gentlemen, this is all we can find
of Mussolini's Abyssinian Empire,
but we think you ought to recognise it!

Lord Halifax Disposes

This is a bitter opposition comment on the British decision to recognize
Italy's conquest of Abyssinia, which was associated with the Anglo–Italian
negotiations.

Foreign Secretary Viscount Halifax addresses the League of Nations,
viewed as a court of law. He displays the mangled remains which are 'all
that we can find of Mussolini's Abyssinian Empire', while Mussolini, in
the bottom right-hand corner, devours the remainder. In the bottom left-
hand corner, ex-Emperor Haile Selassie looks on in dismay.

Cartoon 18.11 Janus 1938. *Marianne*, Paris, 7 December 1938

This French cartoon, drawn towards the end of 1938, takes its title from the two-faced Roman god Janus, and comments on the 'two-faced' attitude of Mussolini. Towards Britain, who had concluded a treaty with Italy, he was all smiles: but towards France he was aggressively hostile. Fascist deputies had recently staged a noisy demonstration demanding Tunisia, Corsica and other French territories.

Marianne looks shocked, but Britannia looks suspicious and truculent. Mussolini, despite his fierce expression, is seen as a mere puppet, whose strings are controlled by Hitler. This magazine's view of the relative importance of Hitler and Mussolini has changed considerably since Cartoon 18.3 was drawn, ten months earlier.

19

Czechoslovakia, 1938

The Austrian *Anschluss* immediately posed deep questions about the future of Czechoslovakia.

The whole of Czechoslovakia had been part of the Austro-Hungarian Empire until 1918, although the western region had belonged to the Austrian section of the empire and the eastern region to the Hungarian. Ethnically, the country was very mixed. Out of a total population of fewer than 15 million, rather less than 50 per cent were Czechs, about 20 per cent were Slovaks, and there were smaller numbers of ethnic Ruthenes, Hungarians and Poles. Immediate attention, however, was drawn to the German-speaking *Sudetendeutsch*, who formed about 23 per cent of the population, and mostly lived on the country's western margin.

Politically, Czechoslovakia was the nearest thing to a democracy in the western sense of the term for a long way in any direction. Its administration was, however, very much concentrated on Prague, and in most matters the Czechs were dominant. Nobody could justly complain of 'persecution', but the non-Czech peoples did sometimes have a legitimate grievance about pro-Czech discrimination.

The *Anschluss* stirred immediate excitement among the *Sudetendeutsch*. At first, there was little formal demand for union with Germany, but Konrad Henlein, the Sudeten leader, expressed a strong demand for autonomy within Czechoslovakia, and for rectification of various other grievances. There could be little doubt that many *Sudetendeutsch*, and probably the large majority of them, desired eventual incorporation within Germany. Indeed, the idea had been bruited at the time of the peace conferences, but was rejected by the Allies.

If the question of the Sudetenland could have been viewed purely on ethnic grounds, without reference to questions of economics, strategy and world politics, the voluntary transfer of the area to Germany might have seemed like a very sensible solution, which would resolve many difficulties for all concerned.

Unfortunately, there were many other considerations involved. The Bohemian mountains formed an excellent natural frontier for Czechoslovakia against Germany (although not against Austria) and were reinforced by strong man-made fortifications. The Czechoslovak economy was operated on the assumption that the Sudetenland was an integral part of the country. And there were immensely important questions of international relations.

A mutual assistance treaty between Czechoslovakia and France dated from 1925. Each country was required to go to the assistance of the other in the event of a German attack which the other resisted. There was also a much newer treaty between Czechoslovakia and the Soviet Union, dating only from 1936. Under this arrangement, if France became involved in war against Germany in support of her treaty with Czechoslovakia, then the Soviet Union was also required to go to Czechoslovakia's assistance.

But how? Today, there is a common frontier between Czechoslovakia and the Soviet Union, but that was not the case in 1938. The only practical route by which the Soviet Union could go to the assistance of Czechoslovakia was through Poland. It was quite plain that Poland would resist any such move by force. Thus the question of what should happen to the Sudetenland was not just a matter for Czechoslovakia and Germany. If for any reason German troops crossed the Czechoslovak frontier, as they had so recently crossed the Austrian frontier, there was a probability of war which would involve Germany, Czechoslovakia, France, the Soviet Union and Poland. In such circumstances, it was very likely that other European countries, including Britain, would eventually become involved, even though they had no immediate treaty obligations in Czechoslovakia's defence.

The overwhelming desire of the British government was to avoid any such development. The best way of preserving peace, so the argument ran, was by Britain using her good offices to encourage an 'internal' solution, acceptable to the Czechoslovak government and to the *Sudetendeutsch*. In that event, neither Germany nor any other country would have cause to intervene.

Britain's international position was such that no other country cared formally to oppose a British initiative in that direction. At first, however, there was little positive response. Then, in July, the British government prevailed upon Viscount (Walter) Runciman to act as 'mediator' in the matter, and upon the others concerned to accept his mediation. Runciman's task was to bring the parties together, not to propose any solution of his own. At first he secured little response, but early in September there did seem some hope that the 'Runciman Mission' might succeed.

But the Runciman Mission failed, and soon there was much violence in the Sudetenland. By mid-September, all chance that the *Sudetendeutsch* could be retained within Czechoslovakia, except perhaps by physical force, had disappeared.

At this point, another piece of alarming news reached the British government. An interview between the British ambassador in Paris and the French Foreign Minister Georges Bonnet created grave doubts about France's disposition to fight, even if the Germans invaded Czechoslovakia.

The meeting, of course, was highly confidential; but the British government could not ignore its implications.

Chamberlain now decided to handle matters himself. He sought an interview with Hitler, to discover just what the Führer's intentions were. There was real doubt on the matter. Did Hitler merely desire incorporation of the Sudetenland in Germany, or did he desire to bring the whole country under his control? Some people even argued that Nazi ideology itself implied that Hitler wished to rule over all 'Germans', but had no wish to rule unwilling Czechs.

At his first interview with Hitler, in Berchtesgaden, Chamberlain got an answer which seemed to mean that Hitler's ambitions were limited to the Sudetenland. But the Sudetenland was not Chamberlain's to give. He managed, however, to bring his Cabinet colleagues and the French round to the idea that it would be in the interest of peace that the Sudetenland should be cut from Czechoslovakia, and eventually – with considerable difficulty – prevailed upon the Czechs to accede to the proposal. All this, too, was highly confidential; but it was leaked to the French press, whereupon an immense furore arose.

Chamberlain met Hitler again at Bad Godesberg, to report back. This time, the Führer was not content with the Sudetenland. Chamberlain, who was well aware that no further concessions were possible, returned home.

For the next few days, war seemed very likely. Then, suddenly, Hitler climbed down. He invited Chamberlain, along with his French counterpart Daladier, and Mussolini, to a conference at Munich. In the British House of Commons, most of the government's opponents, as well as its supporters, responded with eager enthusiasm, although of course there was not the slightest doubt that any peaceful solution would produce the separation of the Sudetenland from Czechoslovakia. Chamberlain had every reason for believing that, if he could secure a settlement by which Czechoslovakia lost no more than the Sudetenland, practically the whole of Britain would support him.

At Munich, Hitler reverted, in effect, to his Berchtesgaden position. The main question was to settle a timetable for the German occupation of the Sudetenland. This was quickly agreed. Hungary and Poland were also making territorial demands against Czechoslovakia. If those demands were not settled between the countries concerned within three months, the four statesmen would meet again. The four powers further agreed to 'guarantee' the remains of Czechoslovakia; but (as was later shown) this term was highly ambiguous in the context, and nobody was at all clear what it meant.

Chamberlain returned to a jubilant London, and Daladier returned to an even more jubilant Paris. The real test of appeasement was now whether the settlement would prove durable.

Cartoon 19.1 Parleur ou haut-parleur? *Marianne*, Paris, 4 May 1938

Parleur ou haut-parleur?

The first clear indication of the demands which the *Sudetendeutsch* were making against the Czechoslovak government was given in a speech by Konrad Henlein at Karlsbad on 24 April 1938.

This French cartoon, 'Spokesman or loud-speaker?', questions what real authority Henlein had. Hitler orates in the background; Henlein mouths the Führer's words in the foreground. Was the '*Sudetendeutsch* problem' an expression of the real concern of the local people, or merely a line of propaganda convenient for Nazi Germany?

The title of the German cartoon opposite can mean either 'Czech economy' or 'Czech pub'. There also seems to be a pun on the double meaning of 'economy'.

Customers representing the various 'minority peoples' of Czechoslovakia – Slovaks, Poles, Hungarians, Ruthenes and Germans – are seated in a beer-hall, and from the expressions on their faces are all dissatisfied

Cartoon 19.2 Tschechische Wirtschaft. *Simplicissimus,* Munich, 22 May 1938

Tschechische Wirtschaft

„Jetzt stellen Sie uns doch endlich was Ordentliches auf den Tisch, Herr Wirt! Bilden Sie sich etwa ein, Sie können heute noch Versailler Urquell verzapfen?!"

with the beverage which the landlord is dispensing from the barrel 'Versailles brew'. 'Versailler Urquell' is a play on the famous Czech 'Pilsner Urquell'. The barrel has been tipped, to enable the landlord to draw the dregs. The Hungarian complains about the drink, which he has evidently knocked over in disgust, and asks whether the landlord still proposes to serve the 'Versailles brew'.

The cartoonist is suggesting that the *Sudetendeutsch* are by no means the only people aggrieved, and that the poor quality of the drink stems from the Versailles settlement.

309

Cartoon 19.3 Czech ... *Daily Herald*, London, 24 May 1938

CZECH—Or Waiting for the Next Move

Puns on the word Czech/check/cheque were innumerable in the period.

This British cartoon appeared during the 'May crisis' of 1938, when – possibly through some misunderstanding of immediate German intentions – the Czechoslovak army was partially mobilized.

The pieces immediately confronting each other are President Beneš of Czechoslovakia and Henlein, the *Sudetendeutsch* leader; but each of them is only part of a larger set. Henlein is backed by German soldiers, Beneš by 'Marianne', Chamberlain and Stalin. The pieces on the far right of the cartoon are contestants in the Spanish Civil War.

<hr>

Hitler, Henlein, and Hodza of Czechoslovakia, are gambling for high stakes over the future of the country in a 'Wild West' saloon, with the questions of the country's 'unity' and the 'autonomy' of the Sudetenland on the table. At least two of the players are armed, which suggests that they contemplate a possible resolution by violence.

Viscount Runciman, carrying a package 'peaceful agreement', seeks to join the party in the hope of removing the threat of a violent outcome.

310

Cartoon 19.4 High stakes. *Punch*, London, 10 August 1938

HIGH STAKES

Daredevil Runciman (to Messrs. Hodza, Henlein and Hitler). "Mind if I take a hand, boys?"

Cartoon 19.5 Vysokaya dogovarnayushchayasya storona. *Izvestiya*, Moscow, 1 September 1938

Высокая договаривающаяся сторона
и л и
твердая позиция господина Генлейна
Рис. Бор. Ефимова.

'High contracting party, or the firm line of Mr Henlein' is the title of this Soviet cartoon. Viscount Runciman, with the words 'Offer of the English Mission of Runciman' on the paper in his hand, which is balanced behind the book 'Concessions', is in serious discussion with the glove-puppet Henlein, who is operated by a sinister-looking Nazi behind the table. The heavy books carry the titles 'Concessions', 'Expertise', 'Draft Agreements' (twice) and 'Investigations'.

The implication is similar to that of the French cartoon (Cartoon 19.1), but more strongly stated: that Henlein had no independent authority in the matter, but was merely a tool of Germany.

Cartoon 19.6 Sur la route de Prague. *Marianne,* 7 September 1938

SUR LA ROUTE DE PRAGUE

– Il y en a des gendarmes dans ce coin-là!

Hitler, the criminal carrying Austria in his bag, is 'on the road to Prague'. The comment, however, is that 'There are gendarmes in these parts!'

The guardians of the law, all of whom carry guns which more than match Hitler's bludgeon, are Premier Daladier of France, Neville Chamberlain and Soviet Foreign Minister Maxim Litvinov. The implication is that they are all resolute, and determined to withstand any attempt which Hitler might make to 'solve' the Czechoslovak problem by force.

In Cartoon 19.7, Runciman is wandering at night 'in the Bohemian forest'. He is confronted by a ghost, who addresses him: 'When you want to know how not to do it, Lord Runciman, then think of me, Woodrow Wilson.'

In this cartoon, the familiar theme that the ills of Europe were largely due to the Versailles settlement, and that Wilson was personally to blame for the worst features of that settlement, is revived. Runciman must at all costs avoid repeating Wilson's errors.

The significance of the abacus which Wilson carries is rather obscure;

Cartoon 19.7 In den böhmischen Wäldern. *Simplicissimus*, Munich, 11 September 1938

In den böhmischen Wäldern

(O. Gulbransson)

"Wenn Sie wissen wollen, wie man 's nicht macht, Lord Runciman, dann denken Sie an mich, Woodrow Wilson!"

perhaps it alludes to the fact that Wilson's career before he entered politics was partly as an academic political economist.

By the time this cartoon appeared, the Runciman Mission was on the verge of final collapse.

Cartoon 19.8 Other hungry ones heard from.
San Francisco Chronicle, 23 September 1938

Other Hungry Ones Heard From

Hitler holds the pie Czechoslovakia and prepares to carve it for himself. Hungary and Poland, each of whom has a substantial ethnic minority in Czechoslovakia, seek a share of the pie.

Slovakia and Ruthenia had both belonged to the Hungarian part of the Austro-Hungarian Empire before 1918. The Hungarians may have hoped for the eventual return of both provinces; they were laying immediate claim to a substantial part of southern Slovakia, where the population was overwhelmingly Magyar. The principal Polish demand was for the coal-producing area of Teschen, which had a mixed population, including many Poles, and had been seized by Czechoslovakia in 1919.

Cartoon 19.9 'Mein Kampf'. *Evening Standard,* 24 September 1938

"MEIN KAMPF"

(Copyright in All Countries)

The title of Hitler's book, 'My struggle', is applied to Chamberlain, who leaves his second meeting with Hitler, at Bad Godesberg, hunched up in gloom, and accompanied by the disconsolate figures of 'Reason' and 'Peace'.

When Chamberlain first met Hitler, at Berchtesgaden, the Führer made demands which eventually Chamberlain was able to satisfy by 'Concessions' – hence the briefcase under the Prime Minister's arm. In spite of these concessions, Hitler made further demands at Godesberg.

In the immediate aftermath of the Godesberg meeting, there was general gloom in Britain. Many people had criticized the original concessions; but even most people who approved of them could see no way of making further concessions. If Hitler continued to press his Godesberg demands, it was difficult to see how war could be avoided. Although Britain had no direct commitment to Czechoslovakia, she could not escape involvement.

Cartoon 19.10 Czech Crisis. *News of the World*, London,
25 September 1938

This cartoon brings out the drama of the situation after Godesberg.
Chamberlain tries desperately to steer the world along the cracking plank
'Czech crisis' from 'chaos' to 'peace': with the jagged rock 'war' just
underneath the plank if he should fail.

There is a little more hope in this cartoon than in the previous one;
but it emphasizes clearly the immense personal responsibility which lay
with Chamberlain in the matter.

Cartoon 19.11 The sigh heard 'round the world. *Los Angeles Times*, 29 September 1938

THE SIGH HEARD 'ROUND THE WORLD!

The title of Cartoon 19.11 is an allusion to 'the shot heard round the world' – the Battle of Lexington, of April 1775, which inaugurated the American War of Independence, and which would be familiar to American readers.

The 'sigh' celebrated in this cartoon was from 'Europe', who read the news of Hitler's 'offer' of a meeting between Chamberlain, Daladier, Mussolini and himself at Munich. The meeting had not yet been held when the cartoon appeared; but it was generally anticipated that a peaceful solution would emerge from it. Although the Munich settlement was later widely and bitterly criticized, the announcement was greeted with immense relief throughout Europe.

'Europe' is removing a gas mask. Poison gas had been extensively used in the First World War, and was the subject of particular horror. Many people thought that it would be used in any future war, and gas masks were prepared for both military and civilian use. As it happened, gas was not used by either side in the Second World War.

Cartoon 19.12 What, no chair for me? *Evening Standard*, London, 30 September 1938

WHAT, NO CHAIR FOR ME ?   *(Copyright in All Countries.)*

This cartoon appeared on the day the Munich meeting was taking place. The four participating statesmen are discussing the map of Czechoslovakia. Stalin appears, and muses on his own exclusion from the conference.

Whether Stalin had any special title to be present is perhaps doubtful; but there were certainly some curious features in the composition of the meeting. Mussolini's presence was rather difficult to explain, for Italy had no immediate interest in Czechoslovakia, and Mussolini, unlike Chamberlain, had played little part in engineering a settlement. More puzzling still was the absence of a representative from Czechoslovakia itself.

At this stage, probably few people bothered who was present or absent, so long as an acceptable and peaceful solution emerged.

Cartoon 19.13 Der Stammtisch. *Völkischer Beobachter, Munich*, 13 October 1938

This cartoon is from an advertisement for a book of sketches which appeared in the principal Nazi newspaper, the *Völkischer Beobachter*, not long after the Munich conference. The 'Stammtisch' of the title is the 'regulars' table', where no stranger would sit without invitation.

The Germans in the strip were eagerly celebrating their government's action at the beginning of the crisis, but became increasingly depressed and dispirited when war seemed likely. Finally, their spirits revived on 1 October when news of the Munich settlement was published.

This cartoon is rather a surprising one for that particular source, for it strongly suggests that there was grave fear and apprehension in Germany at one stage in the crisis – as was certainly the case elsewhere – although the eventual 'solution' was greeted with jubilation.

Der Stammtisch

12. September

21 September

26. September

1. Oktober

20

Aftermath to Munich, 1938–9

The first reaction to the Munich settlement in most countries was one of immense relief. That relief, however, was not universal. Communists everywhere, obedient to the views of the Soviet government, reacted angrily against what they saw as a betrayal of Czechoslovakia. Many other people thought the same. In Britain, the Labour opposition moved a hostile resolution in the House of Commons. Some Conservative politicians were equally critical. Duff Cooper, First Lord of the Admiralty, resigned from the Cabinet in protest. Winston Churchill and Anthony Eden, who were not members of the government, spoke in Parliament in the same vein. In France, the criticism was at first less widespread, save for the Communists, who formed a much more important body in that country than they did in Britain; but soon there were many other French critics. We may speculate how far these various critics believed that Chamberlain and Daladier had acted wrongly at Munich, and how far their real concern was to draw public attention to future dangers.

Some important events followed swiftly on the Munich settlement. Demands were made by the Hungarian and Polish governments for cession of the territories where their respective ethnic minorities lived. The Czechoslovak government acceded to those demands. About the same time, Beneš resigned, and the country was reorganized along lines of regional autonomy. The Czech lands of Bohemia and Moravia in the west, Slovakia in the middle, and tiny Ruthenia in the far east became largely independent. The country's once formidable army was more or less dismantled.

In the weeks which followed Munich, people began to count the cost. The British government soon launched a substantial programme of rearmament – inappropriate, one might say, if they were convinced that peace had been secured. There is some reason for thinking that Hitler, too, was far from pleased on mature reflection. The diplomatic triumph of Munich was considerable; but he may well have believed that – without the Munich settlement – the Czechoslovak state would have collapsed, and its foreign supporters would all have found reasons for not intervening. Nor was Hitler the kind of man to ignore the many bitter things which were said about him in democratic countries in the aftermath of Munich.

The first clear break in the improved diplomatic relations between Germany and the western democracies occurred less than six weeks after Munich. A young Polish Jew had assassinated a German diplomat in Paris. In the early morning of 10 November – *Kristallnacht*, as the occasion was known – the storm broke. Throughout the Reich, synagogues were set on fire and Jewish shops were wrecked. Anti-Semitism had been a feature of Nazi ideology from the start; but with *Kristallnacht* the persecution became much more intense. This behaviour was obviously not the work of local hotheads, but the considered policy of the Nazi state, and it produced the predictable reaction of bitter disgust in the democracies. No further 'appeasement' of Germany could be contemplated for a long time.

In March 1939, the final break came. First the Germans prevailed upon Slovakia to declare its independence. Then the new President and Foreign Minister of Czechoslovakia were summoned to Germany, and were required to accede to the immediate incorporation of Bohemia and Moravia as a 'Protectorate' of the German Reich. The threat of bombardment of Prague a few hours later was held out if they refused. On 15 March, German troops occupied the two western provinces. The eastern province of Ruthenia at first tried to declare independence, but within a couple of days was occupied by Hungary.

The fundamental assumption of appeasement had been that international agreements could be made which would be kept by both sides. The Munich agreement, which had been made by Hitler himself, was broken within six months. There was also the very worrying question: Why did Hitler do it? Economically, Czechoslovakia had been completely at his mercy since Munich. Even Nazi propaganda could hardly discover any remaining military threat. There was a certain amount of plunder to be collected, such as bank gold reserves and military tackle; but this could hardly warrant setting Britain and France by the ears. The only convincing explanation seemed to be that the new arrangement provided a more convenient springboard for new adventures, and particularly for an attack on Poland.

Two days after the seizure of Prague, Chamberlain delivered what could be regarded as public acknowledgement that appeasement was dead. On the following day, 18 March 1939, the British Cabinet met and began to consider how to organize international resistance to Hitler's future designs.

Cartoon 20.1 'I have signed...' *Daily Worker*, London, 1 October 1938

"I HAVE SIGNED EVERYTHING": *Mr. Chamberlain.*

This cartoon appeared in the Communist *Daily Worker* immediately after the Munich agreement. Although the British Communist Party was relatively unimportant – it only had a single MP – the views which it expressed may be taken to be those of the Soviet government and of Communist Parties everywhere.

Chamberlain appears, from the expression on his face, to have been duped completely by Hitler and Mussolini in signing the sinister document which Hitler holds. Daladier is more uncertain about what he had done, but is equally involved, for his signature is also on the paper. Hitler and Mussolini rejoice at the new arrangement.

How far Hitler was really pleased is doubtful. Mussolini had little to rejoice about in the fate of Czechoslovakia, for Italy was gaining nothing from the arrangement, and Germany was becoming relatively much stronger than Italy. The only aspect of the arrangement which could have given him cause for pleasure was the fact that war – for which Italy was totally unprepared – had been averted.

Cartoon 20.2 'Vainqueur à la dernière minute!' *Marianne*, Paris, 5 October 1938

« Vainqueur à la dernière minute ! »

Cartoons 20.2, 20.3 and 20.4 all appeared in the same French periodical within a period of four weeks. The great difference in their tone brings out sharply the way in which ideas changed in what might be called the 'moderate left', both in France and in Britain in the aftermath of Munich.

In the first cartoon, 'Victor at the last minute!', which was drawn immediately after Munich, Chamberlain and Daladier, as the seconds of 'Peace', celebrate her triumph over the prostrate war-god. Hitler walks off with the Sudetenland in the background; but this is seen as a matter of minor importance in comparison with the outcome of the 'match'.

The second cartoon, 'Written on water?', appeared three weeks later. Profound doubts are expressed about the durability of the agreement. Has the word 'peace' been 'written on water'?

Cartoon 20.3 Ecrit sur l'eau? *Marianne*, Paris, 26 October 1938

Ecrit sur L'eau?

In the third cartoon, Daladier, the teacher, confronts his pupil: 'France, here the great problem is stated. You must help me resolve it.' On the blackboard is a grim set of calculations. 'External problem. Third Reich + Italy + Japan = England + France + USSR − Austria − Czechoslovakia. Unknowns: Hungary, Romania, [Yug]oslavia, Poland, USA. Solution urgent.'

The implication seems to be that peace has not been saved at all. The overwhelming problem for France is how to balance world forces to produce the defeat of the perceived enemy.

No great, unpredictable, event had occurred during the period to disturb the first judgement; but people were beginning to take gloomy stock of evidence which had been available all along.

Cartoon 20.4 Daladier . . . *Marianne*, Paris, 2 November 1938

DALADIER. – France, voici posé le grand problème; il faut m'aider à le résoudre . . .

Cartoon 20.5 (see page 328) is also from *Marianne*. 'The rodents' – four of them bearing Nazi swastikas, but the other two labelled 'Poland' and 'Hungary' – gnaw at the edges of Czechoslovakia, from which they have all annexed territory.

There was considerable resentment in the democratic countries at the pressure which Poland and Hungary put on Czechoslovakia to cede the territories in which their own ethnic minorities lived. That pressure had begun before Munich, and it was clearly contemplated at the Munich conference that the pressure would continue and Czechoslovakia would be forced to make concessions.

Cartoon 20.5 Les rongeurs. *Marianne*, Paris, 19 October 1938

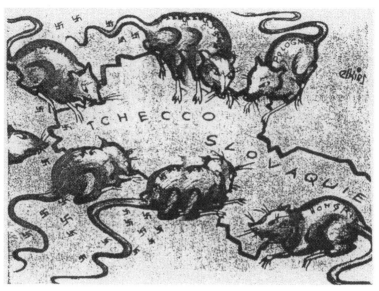

LES RONGEURS

Cartoon 20.6 expresses a German view of three prominent British critics of the Munich agreement: Duff Cooper, who resigned from the Cabinet immediately afterwards, Winston Churchill and Anthony Eden.

The three men are seen as barrage balloons. These balloons were widely used in defence of cities, to compel hostile aircraft to fly at a height where precision bombing was impossible. The object of the 'balloons' in this cartoon, however, is not to dispel enemy raiders, but to repel the doves of peace. The doves, however, are not impeded, as the words at the bottom indicate.

The official line of German propaganda in the immediate aftermath of Munich was that the settlement was a just and reasonable one, which reflected great credit on all four statesmen involved; but that sinister forces were at work which sought to sabotage the arrangement.

It is striking that the three men selected for attack were all dissident Conservatives, although it was the opposition parties who had played the main part in proposing the critical House of Commons motion which was submitted just after Munich. The motion, of course, was easily defeated by the large pro-government majority.

Cartoon 20.6 Cooper, Eden, Churchill. *Simplicissimus,* Munich, 30 October 1938

Cartoon 20.7 Zagrobnoe mnenie. *Izvestiya*, Moscow, 18 November 1938

ЗАГРО НОЕ МНЕНИЕ

Рис. Бор. Ефимова.

ПОСЛЕДНИЙ ЦАРЬ. — Скажу вам по секрету, мой фашистский коллега, меня это не спасло...

These cartoons both refer to the events of '*Kristallnacht*', 10 November 1938, when Nazi persecution of Jews suddenly became much more intense.

In the Soviet cartoon, the Nazi has been assaulting Jews and destroying and looting their property. The ghost of the last Tsar, Nicholas II, appears in the sky, with the words 'Russian monarchy' above his head, and in his hand a list of anti-Jewish 'pogroms' conducted during his reign. The Tsar addresses the Nazi: 'Speaking confidentially, my Fascist colleague, that didn't do me any good . . .'

Before 1917, sporadic pogroms took place in the Russian Empire, with more or less government toleration and even encouragement. Many people

Cartoon 20.8 Oppression and suppression. *Punch*, London,
30 November 1938

OPPRESSION AND SUPPRESSION

Nazi Bully. " My will is the will of Germany ! "

argued that the Tsar's regime was quite pleased that ordinary people should pick on Jews as the scapegoats for sufferings which were really due to the political system ruling the country. The cartoon suggests that, just as these pogroms did not save the Tsar, so also would similar events in Germany fail in the long run to help the Nazis.

The second cartoon, from *Punch*, is perhaps more remarkable, because it appeared in a periodical most of whose readers probably approved strongly of the Munich settlement at the time it was made. Germany is bound and gagged, incapable of expressing the protest she wishes to utter. The 'Nazi bully', with the body of an injured or murdered Jew at his feet, and the fires of '*Kristallnacht*' near by, falsely proclaims his will to be the will of Germany.

This is one of the most pointed anti-Nazi cartoons which had appeared to that date in *Punch*, and provides a remarkable example of the revulsion of British opinion which had taken place only a couple of months after Munich. In this period, and right into the early stages of the Second World War, many British cartoons suggested that the Nazi crimes were in no sense supported by the majority of Germans.

Cartoon 20.9 appeared on 15 March – the Ides of March – 1939, the very day on which German troops marched into Prague, and the truncated Czechoslovak state finally collapsed.

The cartoonist, Sir Bernard Partridge, was also the artist who drew Cartoon 20.8. His drawings were sometimes very perceptive, but on other occasions (as, for example, in Cartoon 12.4) they were profoundly misjudged. In this particular case, his work could hardly have been worse timed. John Bull is by no means unprepared for trouble – as the steel helmet and the paper at his bedside suggest – but the nightmare 'war scare' escapes from the window.

This cartoon had probably been drawn only a few days before it appeared. It is a striking illustration of the very sudden, and generally unexpected, character of the Czechoslovak crisis which took place in March 1939.

Cartoon 20.9 The Ides of March. *Punch*, London, 15 March 1939

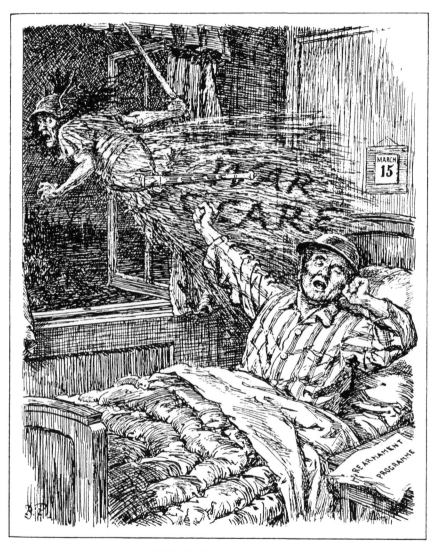

THE IDES OF MARCH

John Bull. "Thank goodness that's over!"

[Pessimists predicted "another major crisis" in the middle of this month.]

333

Cartoon 20.10 'Je suis l'esprit...'. *Le Canard Enchaîné*, Paris, 22 March 1939

— *Je suis l'esprit de Locarno...*
— *...Et moi l'esprit de Munich...*

Two ghosts meet in a cemetery. One introduces himself as 'the spirit of Locarno'. The other replies by describing himself as 'the spirit of Munich'.

Just as the cooperative 'spirit of Locarno' - which seems to be carrying a dove – is dead, so also is the 'spirit of Munich' and the associated idea of appeasement. The 'spirit of Munich' has a different kind of bird, probably a crow, on its shoulder. A crow is an unpopular bird, for it does damage, has unattractive plumage, makes an unpleasant noise and is not good to eat. In colloquial French, perhaps relevant here, *un corbeau* is an undertaker's man. The owl, sitting on the tombstone in the background, is widely regarded as a bird of ill omen.

This cartoon appeared in a weekly periodical just seven days after the seizure of Prague. In France, as in Britain, that event was taken as proof positive that appeasement was dead.

Cartoon 20.11 Step on it. *Star*, London, 22 March 1939

These two British cartoons, Cartoons 20.11 and 20.12, appeared shortly after the seizure of Prague.

The message of 'Step on it' is one of urgency. The Nazi tank is advancing. Will Britain, France and the Soviet Union 'put their foot down' - in both senses of the term? The implication is that they must both adopt a firm policy and stamp on the Nazi war machine. The suggestion seems to be that immediate action will be both simple and effective.

The second cartoon (see page 336) is another Partridge drawing, and this time his generally good judgement has returned. The false pledges and the propaganda investing the Nazi dragon 'Aggression' are dissipating. St George eyes the creature, which he realizes he must probably fight to the death.

The use of the English patron saint to represent Britain, or the United Kingdom, would probably be resented today by the people of Scotland and Wales; but in the 1930s the assumption of English primacy was less frequently challenged.

Cartoon 20.12 St George and the dragon. *Punch*, London,
29 March 1939

ST. GEORGE AND THE DRAGON: THE SMOKE-SCREEN CLEARS.

21

The road to war,
March–September 1939

In the immediate aftermath of the German seizure of Bohemia and Moravia, two more territorial changes took place. Germany required Lithuania to cede the port of Memel, now Klaipèda. Memel had belonged to Germany before 1919, when it was created a Free City; but it was later seized by Lithuania. On 22 March 1939, agreement was reached between the two countries, by which the city was restored to Germany. The transfer took place without too much ill-will, and Lithuania was permitted to use facilities of the port.

The second change affected Albania. The country had long been an economic dependency of Italy, but on 7 April – Good Friday – Italian troops invaded the country, and in a short time completed annexation.

These events were not ignored – Chamberlain in particular resented the seizure of Albania – but they were seen as something apart from the mainstream of international politics. It was taken almost for granted that further major acts of German aggression were planned. The overriding question was what action should be taken to contain such aggression. With almost universal support at home, the British government took it upon itself to organize international resistance. At first it was not clear which country was the next intended victim; but it soon became clear that the most likely country was Poland. The amputation of the 'Polish Corridor' and the town of Danzig (Gdansk) under the peace treaties was particularly resented in Germany.

The British idea was to establish some sort of treaty with France, Poland and the Soviet Union, by which the four countries would agree to stand together and fight against future German aggression. This immediately ran into difficulties. France was glad enough to join; but there was trouble with both Poland and the Soviet Union. Not all the difficulties became apparent immediately. The Soviet Union feared that it would bear the brunt of any fighting which might take place, and it also required access to other places – notably to parts of Poland and to the Baltic states. The Poles, who had good historical reason for thinking that the Russians would be exceedingly difficult to remove at a later date, were most anxious that this should not happen. They also had some fear that too close an association with the Soviet Union would actually provoke a German attack.

While the British were looking for some kind of compromise which would be acceptable to both Poland and the Soviet Union, reports arrived in London which suggested that Germany was putting immediate pressure on Poland, and that almost any day Poland would be forced either to make great concessions or else be invaded by Germany. These reports were probably wrong; but the British government was taking no chances. On 31 March, the celebrated British 'guarantee' to Poland was issued.

How, one might ask, could the British 'guarantee' Poland, in any meaningful sense of the word? Britain had few or no forces which she could despatch to Poland. About all that could be said was that a German attack on Poland would constitute a *casus belli* for Britain. As France already had her treaty with Poland – albeit somewhat crumpled over the years – a German move in that direction would, in theory at least, involve Britain and France in war.

But what of the Soviet Union? Throughout the spring and summer, negotiations between Britain and the USSR proceeded. At first, it looked as if some way would be found to circumvent the various difficulties and complete the alliance. As time went on, however, the prospect gradually became less bright. Early in May, Litvinov was replaced by Vyacheslav Molotov as Commissar for Foreign Affairs. Still the negotiations proceeded, but nothing emerged. The Soviet negotiators questioned the British bona fides; the British considered that impossible conditions were being demanded.

Meanwhile, Molotov was thinking of other ways in which his country's interest might be advanced. On 21 August, the world was astonished to learn that a Non-aggression Pact between the Soviet Union and Germany was planned. Two days later, the agreement was signed. On the face of it, it was little more than an agreement that the two countries would not attack each other; but in practice there was a great deal more behind it. It certainly meant that Germany could attack Poland without involving the Soviet Union as an enemy.

In the ensuing week, there were innumerable frantic negotiations. At bottom, the Germans probably thought that Britain and France were bluffing. Surely they would not fight if no vital interest of their own was involved? And, furthermore, the Soviet Union would not intervene. Very probably, the Nazi leadership simply did not understand the element of moral fury and public determination which had been aroused. The democracies, for their part, were particularly anxious to dispel such misunderstanding – not least because many people had long argued that misunderstanding of intentions had played a large part in bringing the powers to war in 1914. As a sort of diplomatic signal, the British guarantee to Poland was rapidly converted into a full-blown treaty, and every effort was made to state intentions as clearly as possible.

All in vain. On 1 September, Germany attacked Poland. Further frantic diplomacy followed. The French government hesitated, which was probably what Hitler had anticipated. Mussolini, whose country was still completely unprepared for war, and who (like the Japanese) was far from pleased with the German–Soviet Non-aggression Pact, attempted to stop the war. The British government saw that there was no way out. Even so, many people on all sides in Parliament felt and expressed doubts about the government's intentions. These doubts were misplaced, but their expression probably hastened events a little. At 11 a.m. on Sunday 3 September, Britain was at war with Germany, and at 5 p.m. of the same day France followed.

Cartoon 21.1 . . . Loves me, loves me not . . . Evening Standard, London, 15 April 1939

. . . LOVES ME, LOVES ME NOT . . .   *(Copyright in All Countries.)*

This cartoon comments on the Italian seizure of Albania. The 'Anglo–Italian Pact', which Chamberlain holds, had been reached in principle in April 1938, and formally completed in the following November.

Using the 'Pact' as a flower from which an uncertain lover detaches successive petals ('She loves me, she loves me not'), Chamberlain attempts to ascertain whether Mussolini still 'loves him'.

The recent Italian adventure strongly suggested the contrary. In the shrubbery nearby is an even clearer answer: Mussolini is in happy embrace with Hitler.

The cartoon opposite appeared just after Easter 1939.

The litter which is commonly generated on such occasions is compared with the litter of international agreements which was associated, first with the German seizure of western Czechoslovakia, and then – even more recently – with the Italian invasion of Albania. 'Pledged word', 'Treaties',

Cartoon 21.2 After the holiday. *Daily Express*, London, 11 April 1939

AFTER THE HOLIDAY

'Assurances', 'Peace Pact' and specifically 'Munich Agreement' are scattered on the ground, and 'Peace' is left with the task of clearing the mess.

If some treaties had been violated with impunity, why should others be secure? The 'sanctity' of international agreements, unlike the 'sanctity' of private contracts, does not turn on the existence of courts of law to which an aggrieved party may turn and which have the power to enforce their judgments. Instead, that 'sanctity' turns upon a general appreciation that if a state reneges on one agreement, all other treaties which it has made are devalued, which discourages others from entering agreements with that country, preferring to make agreements with people whom they trust more. When many treaties are broken, and by several parties, this kind of sanction begins to break down, and the temptation is for others also to break treaties. If treaties are not honoured, then the only other way of regulating international relations is by war or threat of war. That was happening in 1939, which may be the reason why the burden of disposing of the mess, as seen in this cartoon, lay with 'Peace'.

Cartoon 21.3 A l'est, du nouveau! *Marianne*, Paris, 12 April 1939

A L'EST, DU NOUVEAU!

'In the east now!' is a French comment on the British decision to guarantee Poland.

The shadow of Hitler approaches the Polish Corridor. Signs are posted in German and French, saying 'Entry forbidden'. The signs are supported on rolled umbrellas. An umbrella was commonly associated with Neville Chamberlain in contemporary cartoons.

Cartoon 21.4 L'école de M. Beck. *Le Canard Enchaîné,* Paris, 3 May 1939

L'ECOLE DE M. BECK

Je ne tolérerai pas d'autostrade dans mon corridor !

In the period immediately after the British guarantee to Poland, more or less informal German government approaches were made to the Polish government, suggesting some kind of 'compromise' over the 'Polish Corridor' question. One such idea was that there should be a plebiscite in the Corridor; that the 'winner' should get the Corridor, but the 'loser' should be empowered to build an *Autobahn* – roughly, a motorway – across it. If Germany were the loser this would link the bulk of the country with East Prussia; if Poland were the loser it would give Poland a route to the sea. These suggestions were probably not made with any real conviction, or even hope, that there was any chance of their being taken up.

The title of this cartoon, 'The school of M. Beck', refers to Colonel Beck, Foreign Minister of Poland. The word 'school' is used both literally and metaphorically. The school cleaner reprimands two small boys who are playing with cars and scooters, 'I won't tolerate a motorway in my corridor!'

Cartoon 21.5 M. Strang à Moscou. *Le Canard Enchaîné*, Paris, 21 June 1939

M. STRANG A MOSCOU

— Allo ? London ?
Tout va bien...

„,.le pacte, elle était
sur le point...

...d'être signé...

This cartoon appeared in the second half of June 1939, and comments on the slow progress of the Anglo–Soviet negotiations, which were designed to achieve some kind of common front against future German expansion.

Conduct of negotiations on such an important matter would normally be handled by an ambassador, or even by a senior member of the government. On this occasion, however, the British ambassador to Moscow had been temporarily recalled to London, where he developed influenza and was unfit to travel. A senior Foreign Office official, William Strang, was sent in his place. Some Soviet sympathizers in Britain represented this as an insult to the Soviet Union. Negotiations continued nevertheless, but were ineffectual.

In the first frame of this cartoon, Strang happily reports to London that 'all is going well'. In the second and third frames, a progressively ageing Strang reports that the pact 'is on the point of being signed'.

The cartoon opposite, which appeared on Midsummer Day, parodies the play-within-a-play *Pyramus and Thisbe* in Shakespeare's *Midsummer Night's Dream*.

The two doomed lovers are Chamberlain (complete with umbrella) as Pyramus and the USSR as Thisbe. Pyramus seeks a chink in the wall, which performs an active part in the play. The wall is the Baltic States problem.

As Anglo–Soviet negotiations proceeded, the Soviet Union pressed for Britain to authorize what was, in effect, Soviet authority to intervene if necessary in the affairs of Estonia, Latvia and Lithuania. Britain refused to accede. Whether the Soviet government anticipated any different result seems most doubtful.

Cartoon 21.6 A Midsummer Day's plea. *Punch*, London, 21 June 1939

A MIDSUMMER DAY'S PLEA

Pyramus. "Thou wall, O wall, O sweet and lovely wall,
Show me thy chink." ("*A Midsummer Night's Dream*" Act V Sc. 1)

[Mr. CHAMBERLAIN recently referred to "a sort of wall between the British and Russian Governments which it is extremely difficult to penetrate."]

Cartoon 21.7 Still on the doorstep. *Evening Standard*,
London, 5 July 1939

STILL ON THE DOORSTEP   *(Copyright in All Countries.)*

In the period after Munich, and particularly after the seizure of Prague, substantial pressure built up in favour of changes in the British government. The immediate demand was not for the establishment of an administration of a radically different political complexion, but rather the incorporation of certain critics within the existing National Government.

Few members of the opposition parties had great personal prestige – Lloyd George was the great exception here, but many people disliked him, and he was judged by others to be too old. There was, however, a powerful argument for incorporating some Conservative critics who had held high office in the past, but who for one reason or another had fallen foul of the existing leadership. Of those people, Winston Churchill and Anthony Eden attracted special attention. Churchill had long been a particularly trenchant and well-informed critic of appeasement.

In this cartoon of July 1939, 'Public Opinion' hammers on the door of 10 Downing Street, with Churchill and Eden waiting beside him.

Cartoon 21.8 Safety first! *Punch*, London, 30 August 1939

SAFETY FIRST!

This cartoon comments on the German–Soviet Non-aggression Pact of August 1939.

Hitler and his Foreign Minister von Ribbentrop are in a sleigh, pursued by a pack of wolves. Ribbentrop hurls out the baby 'Anti-Communism', with Hitler's book *Mein Kampf* attached, in the hope of placating the wolves and permitting the occupants of the sleigh to escape to safety.

The Non-aggression Pact, which seemed on its face a tremendous diplomatic coup by the Nazis – and possibly by the Soviet government as well – was generally represented in Britain as a great concession by the German government, and a mark of deep apprehension at the mounting strength and determination of the future Allies.

Apparently wolves seldom or never behave in the manner suggested in the cartoon; but few people in Britain at that time knew much about the habits of wild animals.

Cartoon 21.9 'There's some mistake . . .' *Daily Express,* London, 6 September 1939

"THERE'S SOME MISTAKE, IT WAS YOUR SMALL BROTHER I SENT FOR".

This cartoon appeared just after the Second World War began. Hitler, in his study at Berchtesgaden, has summoned Mars's 'small brother'; but the great war-god appears in person, and towers over the dictator.

The cartoonist suggests that Hitler had planned a small war against Poland, but discovered to his astonishment and dismay that he has conjured up a very big war against Britain and France.

There is some reason for thinking that Hitler really did believe that he would be able to fight and win a war against Poland without Britain and France intervening. In one sense he was right, for although they both declared war on 3 September, neither played an important part in rendering either direct or indirect assistance to the Poles. In a more important sense he was profoundly wrong, for neither country showed any disposition to withdraw from the conflict once Poland had been defeated.

22

Reflections

This cartoon appeared on the day after Britain and France declared war on Germany.

The character 'History' appears repeatedly in the *Chicago Tribune* as a wise, often sad, old man. Here History leans on his huge, bloodstained volume, in despair at the continuing human folly signalled by the outbreak of the new war. No particular individual or country is selected for blame; the responsibility is universal.

That judgement becomes more and more convincing as the events recede from us. As many cartoons in this book have shown, it was not likely to prove a popular view at the end of the 1930s. Most people found it much easier to select some particular target for blame. It was very easy, for example, to point out that Hitler or Stalin were exceptionally wicked men, and the world today may take some comfort from the fact that the countries where they were once afforded almost divine honours are now in the forefront of those exposing their crimes. Other commentators chose for especial blame people whom no one would describe as monsters, but whose judgement has been profoundly criticized: Chamberlain or Lloyd George; Clemenceau or Poincaré; Hindenburg or Wilson.

The view that the world went to war because Hitler and Stalin were psychopaths is less than adequate as an explanation of events. Every society contains its potential Hitlers and Stalins. Far more numerous than these monsters are people who are in no sense egregiously evil, but whose judgement is gravely at fault. A healthy nation, a healthy world, can cope with the damage done by both groups of people. The world of the 1930s was profoundly unhealthy, not just in one respect but in many.

'Will they never . . . never learn?' bewails History in our cartoon. Since that cartoon was drawn, some lessons do seem to have been learnt by thinking people in all lands. 'The futility of war', which History was particularly anxious to teach, is now understood a good deal more widely than it was in 1939, although part of the reason is that weapons have increased immeasurably in their destructive power since that date.

People have also learnt some 'lessons of history' about the way in which wars happen. Economic nationalism is now much less widespread than it was in 1939, but it is by no means dead, and 'economic regionalism' is still very much alive, and a powerful cause of ill-feeling. 'Racism', which

Cartoon 22.1 Lessons of history. *Chicago Tribune,* 4 September 1939

was such a potent force in 1939, and was then often accepted by relatively educated people, is today a term of contempt for prejudices which are held mainly by the ignorant and stupid. 'Nationalism' has not yet followed 'racism' into a sort of moral limbo, but the idea that some particular national community posesses an exceptional share of either good or bad qualities is gradually receding to the 'lunatic fringe'. Unfortunately, opinion is still a long way from acknowledging that all people everywhere have an equal right of access to the world's natural resources, with an equal duty to care for those resources. When we reach that point, the deepest of all the causes of war will have been removed. The world has learnt quite a lot since 1939, but History still has much to teach us. There is some reason for believing that one day we may prove more apt pupils than people were in the past.

A glance at the cartoons in this book shows how easily the racist or nationalist notions were preserved. Again and again we find illustrations which either personalized nations through allegorical figures – Uncle Sam, John Bull, Marianne, Michel and so on – or which represented some political leader as the epitome of his nation. Once people began to think of one individual, whether actual or allegorical, as the spokesman not just of a government but of a whole people, the road was open for those who hated the activities of that individual to see everybody living in the country which he 'represented' as a participant in his crimes or follies.

These cartoons bring out a serious danger to clear thought. A cartoonist necessarily exaggerates and over-simplifies situations, and tends to polarize opinion. It is very easy for a reader, especially for a reader who desires a neat 'explanation' which confirms his prejudices, to see matters in the over-simplified manner of the cartoonist's presentation, and to convince himself that this highly subjective view is no more than objective reality. When Weimar Germany still had a healthy democracy, the Nazis were seen in most German cartoons as something ridiculous, and their ideology was lampooned. There were real danger signs when the German cartoonists began to take Nazi ideology as a rational view of the world. Soviet cartoons bring out a similar point. By making a figure look brutal, or by sticking a swastika or the label 'Fascist' upon him, they could easily incite hatred among their readers. On the whole, cartoons from the democratic countries were more subtle; but even in those it is often worthwhile noting facial expressions which prompt sympathy or antipathy as important features in the propagandist's art.

Yet the cartoonist often played a very positive role. He could sometimes cut through a great deal of confusion and obfuscation to reach the heart of an issue. He could ridicule the deeds and ideas of powerful men, and make them seem absurd as well as wicked. Some of the inter-war cartoonists were very clever men indeed, who were able to put their fingers upon problems far more effectively than most of the contemporary politicians. It is arguable, for example, that some cartooonists played a really significant part in alerting British people to the true character of Hitler.

Whatever function the inter-war cartoonist played for contemporaries, his role today is entirely positive. He casts much light on the outlook not only of the people he drew, but also of the people for whom he drew: their weaknesses and strength; their folly and their wisdom; the assumptions of the societies in which they lived. This greatly enhances understanding of the period: what it was that made people act as they did; what constraints there were on the actions of political leaders; why human beings not wildly different from ourselves, or from each other, became locked in a war in which forty or fifty million of them died.

This is helpful not only in understanding the past but also in understanding the present. Because a mixed collection of international cartoons compels the reader to look at problems not just from one viewpoint but from many, people are disposed to recognize the 'many-sidedness of truth'. Perhaps this attitude will play some small part in reducing the risk of major conflicts in the future.